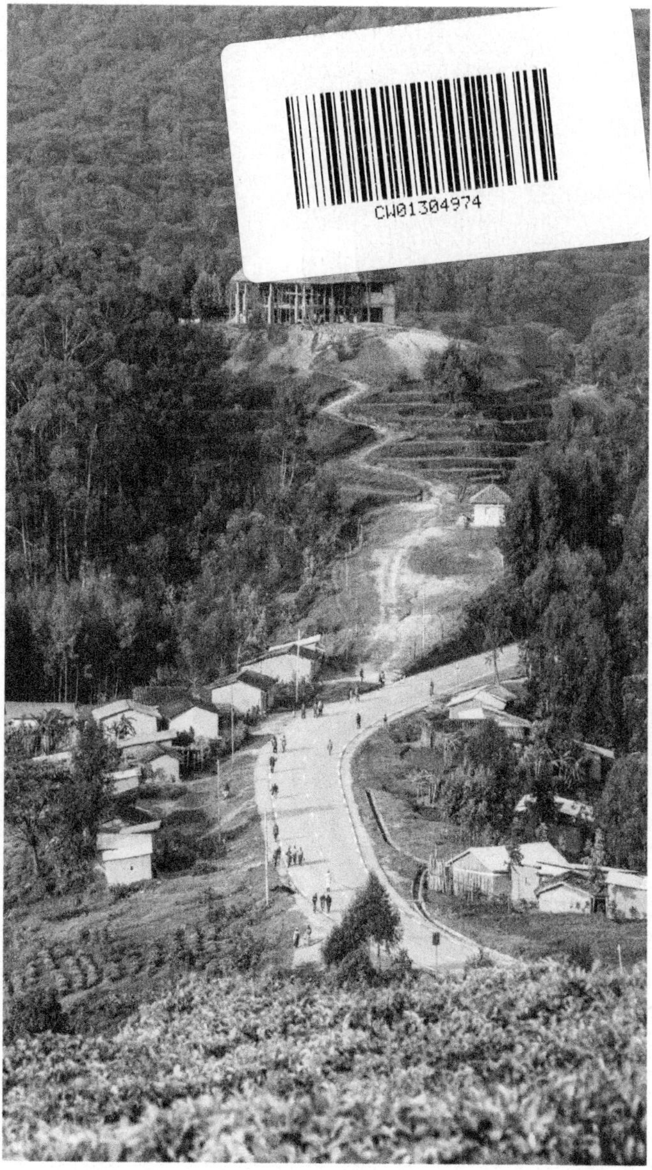

CW01304974

Uganda & Rwanda Travel Guide 2024

Gorillas, Volcanoes, Wildlife & More: the Pearl of Africa & The Land of a Thousand Hills

Curtis Kerr

© 2024 Curtis Kerr

All rights reserved. No part of this publication may be reproduced, distributed, or transmitted in any form or by any means, including photocopying, recording, or other electronic or mechanical methods, without the prior written permission of the publisher, except in the case of brief quotations embodied in critical reviews and certain other noncommercial uses permitted by copyright law.

Disclaimer:

While every effort has been made to ensure the accuracy and completeness of the information in this book, the author and publisher cannot be held responsible for any errors, omissions, or changes that may occur after publication.

Travel advice and recommendations are subject to change due to various factors, including weather conditions, seasonal fluctuations, business closures, and cultural considerations. Readers are encouraged to undertake their research and verify information independently before making travel decisions.

The use of any information or advice contained within this book is at the reader's own risk. Neither the author nor the publisher are liable for any damages or losses arising from the use of information in this book.

This book is intended for informational purposes only and should not be interpreted as professional advice. For matters related to legal, financial, or healthcare concerns, please consult with qualified professionals.

By using this book, you agree to these terms and conditions.

Happy Exploring!

Contents

Part 1: Planning Your Trip

Chapter 1: Welcome to the Pearl of Africa and the Land of A Thousand Hills.

1.1 Uganda: Introducing a Land of Diverse Beauty.

1.2 Rwanda: Where Nature Meets Culture.

Chapter 2: When to Visit and What to Bring

2.1 Best Time to Visit Uganda: The Land of Eternal Spring

2.2 Best Time to Visit Rwanda: The Land of a Thousand Hills and Diverse Delights.

2.3 Packing Essentials for Uganda & Rwanda: Ready for Adventure

Chapter 3: Visas and Permits: Unlocking the Gates of Adventure (Without the Headache)

3.1 Visa Requirements for Uganda: The Pearl of Africa is Awaiting!

3.2 Visa Requirements in Rwanda: The Land of a Thousand Hills Welcomes You

3.3 Getting Gorilla Trekking Permits: Face-to-Face with Gentle Giants (But Remember the Permit!)

Chapter 4: Getting There and Getting Around: Conquering the Sky and Hitting the Road (Without Getting Lost)

4.1 Flights to Uganda and Rwanda: Soaring Like an Eagle (Without Feathered Wings)

4.2 Transportation Options in Uganda: Driving Ugandan-Style

4.3 Transportation Options in Rwanda: Exploring Rwanda by Wheels

Chapter 5: Health & Safety: Keep You Adventuring Worry-Free (Without the Drama)

5.1 Recommended Vaccinations for Uganda and Rwanda: Staying Healthy (and Adventure-Ready)

5.2 Travel Insurance Considerations: Peace of Mind for the Unexpected.

Chapter 6: Money Matters: Making Your Ugandan Shillings Stretch Further Than a Yogi (Without Breaking the Bank)

6.1 Currency Exchange in Uganda and Rwanda: Don't Be a "Mzungu" with Money Problems ("Mzungu" is a Kiswahili name for foreigner)

6.2 Budgeting Tips for Your Trip: Ballin' on a Budget (Without Feeling Like a Cheapskate).

Chapter 7: Language and Culture: Bridging the Gap (Without Any Faux Pas).

7.1 Essential Phrases in English, Luganda (Uganda), and Kinyarwanda.

7.2 Understanding Ugandan and Rwandan Culture: A Crash Course (With a Personal Story About a Goat)

Part 2: Exploring Uganda
Chapter 8:Kampala:The beautiful capital of Uganda

    8.1 Must-See Sights in Kampala: A Sensory Delight for the Adventurous Soul

    8.2 Cultural Experiences in Kampala: Introducing the Ugandan Soul

Chapter 9: Bwindi Impenetrable National Park: Tracking Gentle Giants (Without Annoying Them)

    9.1 Gorilla Trekking Permits and Booking Information: Don't Be Shut Out (by a Gorilla or Park Ranger)

    9.2 What to Expect on a Gorilla Trek: Prepare for Adventure (and Perhaps a Little Mud).

    9.3 Responsible Gorilla Trekking Practices: Be a Force of Good (Not a Banana-Tossing Tourist)

Chapter 10: Queen Elizabeth National Park: Where Wildlife Roams Free (And Might Steal Your Breakfast)

    10.1 Wildlife Viewing in Queen Elizabeth National Park: Spotting Everything From Lions to Tree-Climbing Lions.

    10.2 Kazinga Channel Boat Cruise: A Hippo Haven with Unexpected Encounters

    10.3 Accommodation Options Near Queen Elizabeth National Park: Relaxing After a Day of Wildlife Encounters.

Chapter 11: Beyond the Parks: Revealing Uganda's Soul (and Perhaps Mastering the Art of Matoke)

11.1 Homestay Experiences in Rural Uganda: A Hilarious Immersion (and Perhaps a Few Mosquito Bites).

11.2 Traditional Ugandan Crafts and Souvenirs: Beyond the T-Shirt

11.3 Experiencing Ugandan Cuisine & Cooking Classes: A Culinary Adventure (with Maybe a Little Spice)

Part 3: Exploring Rwanda

Chapter 12: Kigali: A Modern City Rich in History

12.1 Kigali Genocide Memorial & Learning about Rwanda's Past: A Journey of Remembrance (and Perhaps Some Tears)

12.2 Museums and Cultural Sites in Kigali: Exploring Rwandan History and Creativity

12.3 Exploring Kigali's Art Scene and Restaurants: A Feast for the Senses

Chapter 13: Volcanoes National Park: Mountain Gorilla Trekking in the Mist!

13.1 Gorilla Trekking Permits and Booking Information: Securing Your Once-in-a-Lifetime Experience

13.2 What to Expect on a Gorilla Trek in Volcanoes National Park: An Experience Like No Other

13.3 Responsible Gorilla Trekking Practices: Be a Force of Good

Chapter 14: Nyungwe Forest National Park: Discovering a Realm of Emerald Magic

14.1 Chimpanzee Tracking Permits and Booking Information: Meeting Our Closest Cousins

14.2 Exploring the Nyungwe Forest Canopy Walk: A Bird's Eye View of the Rainforest

14.3 Biodiversity and Wildlife Viewing in Nyungwe National Park: A Land of Riches

Chapter 15: Akagera National Park: Wildlife Safaris in Rwanda's Savannah

15.1 Wildlife Viewing Opportunities in Akagera National Park: A feast for the eyes.

15.2 Game Drives and Safaris in Akagera National Park: Discovering the Wild

15.3 Park Entrance Fees and Booking Information

15.4 Accommodation Options Near Akagera National Park.

Chapter 16: Genocide Memorials and Cultural Sites: Reflecting on Rwanda's Past

16.1 Kigali Genocide Memorial: A Place of Remembrance (A Journey Through History and Emotion)

16.2 Additional Genocide Memorial Sites in Rwanda

16.3 Cultural Experiences in Rwanda: Beyond the Shadow of History.

Chapter 17: Accommodation Options (Budget to Luxury): Find Your Rwandan Refuge

17.1 Budget Accommodation Options in Uganda and Rwanda: Keeping it Simple but Comfortable

17.2 Mid-Range Accommodation Options in Uganda and Rwanda: Achieving the Ideal Balance

17.3 Luxury Lodges & Camps in Uganda & Rwanda: Unforgettable Experiences in Unique Style

Chapter 18: Dining: A Culinary Adventure Through Uganda and Rwanda.

18.1 Must-Try Ugandan Dishes: A Fusion Of Flavors

18.2 Must-Try Rwandan Dishes: Celebrating Freshness

18.3 Vegetarian and Vegan Dining Options: A World of Flavor Awaits.

Chapter 19: Staying Connected (Internet Access and Phone Usage)

19.1 Internet Access and SIM Card Options: Connecting with the World

19.2 Staying Connected with Phone Calls and Texting: Keeping in Touch

Chapter 20: Sustainable Travel Tips: Making a Positive Impact in Rwanda

Bonus Chapter: Adventures and Itineraries.

Chapter 21: Suggested Itineraries
    21.1 Short Uganda Adventure (3-5 Day):
    21.2 Uganda Wildlife and Gorilla Safari (7-10 Days):
    21.3 Best of Uganda and Rwanda (10-14 Days)
    21.4 Rwanda: Volcanoes and Cultural Immersion (5-7 Days)
    21.5 Multi-Country East African Adventure (Optional: Includes Kenya or Tanzania)

Appendix
    1: Maps of Uganda and Rwanda.
    2:   Glossary of Terms

Hello there, fellow explorer!

As a travel writer with a severe case of wanderlust, I've chased sunsets across continents, kayaked across turquoise seas, and bargained-for colorful treasures in crowded markets. But there's something unique about East Africa, a country that has burrowed its way deep into my heart and refused to let go.

Remember that National Geographic program you saw as a youngster when the stately silverback gorilla softly cradled its young? Imagine yourself being only feet away from these incredible animals in Uganda's Bwindi Impenetrable National Park. The mist hanging to the green canopy, the quiet moans reverberating through the old jungle, it's an experience that will leave you speechless (and possibly racing for your camera!).

But Uganda and Rwanda are much more than simply gorillas. Imagine standing on the lip of the enormous Murchison Falls, where the Nile River thunders down a 146-foot plunge, unleashing a spray that dances with rainbows. Imagine yourself pursuing playful chimps through the lush woods of Kibale National Park, their hoots and shouts filling the air.

Rwanda, dubbed the **"Land of a Thousand Hills,"** has its sort of charm. I vividly recall the exhilaration of climbing through the volcanic Virunga Massif, the air crisp and thin, and snow-capped peaks in the distance. Then there's the lush Nyungwe Forest National Park, which is home to chimps and colobus monkeys and offers a thrilling canopy walk high above the forest floor.

Beyond the environmental attractions, Uganda and Rwanda have thriving civilizations waiting to be discovered. Imagine drinking a steamy cup of Ugandan coffee at a roadside shop or discovering the mysteries of Rwanda's complex basket-weaving heritage. The friendliness and generosity of the people here are as memorable as the surroundings.

This booklet is your key to experiencing the charm of Uganda and Rwanda. I've put my experiences, practical suggestions, and hidden treasures onto these pages to help you create your unique vacation. So, pack your luggage, bring your sense of wonder, and prepare to be astounded!

Thank you for picking this guide as your travel companion. Let the exploration begin!

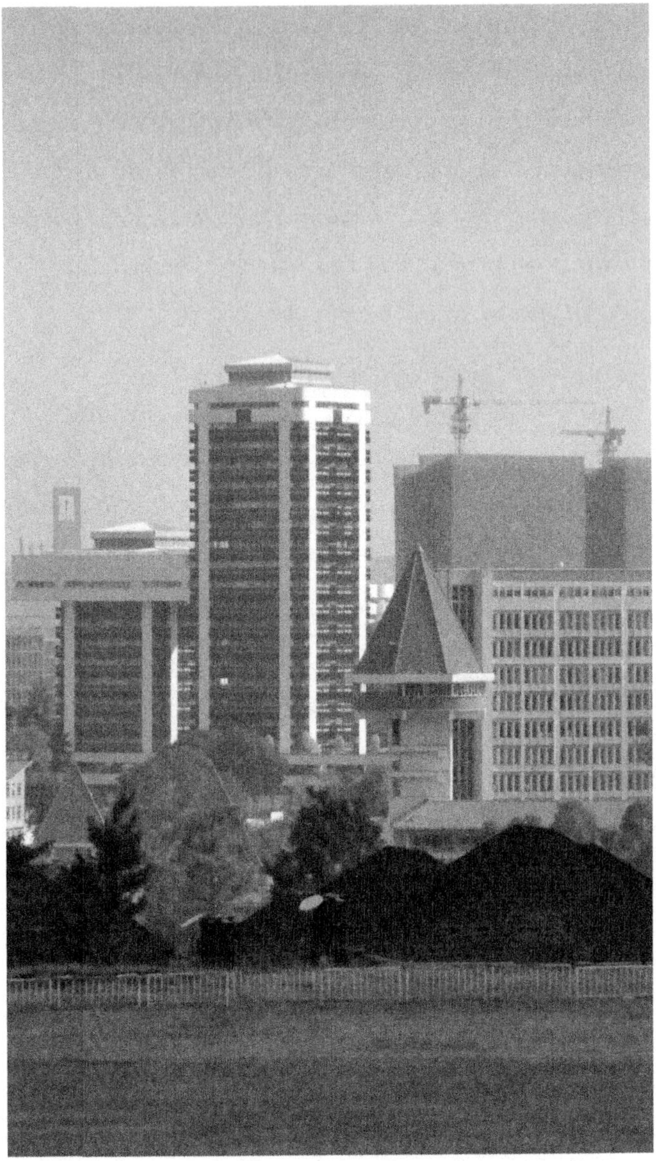

Part 1

Planning Your Trip

Chapter 1: Welcome to the Pearl of Africa and the Land of A Thousand Hills.

Buckle up; adventure awaits! This handbook is your ticket to discovering the wonder of Uganda and Rwanda, two East African nations that will leave you breathless (and with a camera roll full of unforgettable memories).

1.1 Uganda: Introducing a Land of Diverse Beauty.

Uganda, dubbed the "Pearl of Africa" by none other than the great Sir Winston Churchill, is a stunning mix of landscapes, cultures, and animal encounters. Imagine snow-capped mountains scraping the sky in the Rwenzori Ranges, called the "Mountains of the Moon" by Ptolemy, a 2nd-century Greek astronomer (guess they didn't have Google Maps then!).

Descend from those towering heights and you'll find yourself surrounded by verdant rainforests alive with life, wide savannas studded with grazing zebras and lumbering elephants, and the great Nile River winding its way through the center of the nation.

History fans, prepare for a time warp! Uganda has a rich and intriguing history. The ancient Bunyoro kingdom, once a regional superpower, created remarkable earthworks that demonstrated their creativity. Fast forward a few decades and you'll come across the fascinating account of British explorer John Speke, who discovered the source of the Nile River near Lake Victoria in 1858 (it turns out it wasn't precisely where everyone believed it was!).

Today, Uganda is a dynamic country full of kind people. Expect lively conversation at roadside marketplaces brimming with colorful textiles and locally made gifts. You could even get a glimpse of the national pastime: people holding jerry cans on their heads with an almost superhuman sense of balance (don't attempt this at home!).

1.2 Rwanda: Where Nature Meets Culture.

Rwanda, often known as the "***Land of a Thousand Hills,***" is a patchwork of magnificent beauty, ancient traditions, and a strong sense of endurance. Consider this: volcanoes penetrate the skies, their slopes covered in lush forests filled with wildlife. Then there are the undulating hills, each with its narrative to be told.

Rwanda's cultural legacy is just as vivid as its scenery. The exquisite technique of basket weaving, handed down through generations, exemplifies the nation's inventiveness. The rhythmic thrumming of drums and the beautiful movements of traditional dancers will have you tapping your feet and swaying your hips (don't worry, there's no need to participate, but feel free to let loose if the music touches you!).

Despite a difficult history, Rwanda has risen with unflinching strength and a vision for the future. The nation is a pioneer in conservation initiatives, and its dedication to sustainability is admirable. So, when you're here, don't be shocked to see eco-friendly resorts and responsible tourism efforts; it's all part of the Rwandan experience.

Now, here's the greatest part: you get to do all of this and more! *This handbook is your reliable friend, providing information to assist you traverse crowded cities, isolated villages, and untamed nature. So prepare to go on your own Ugandan and Rwandan adventure, complete with jaw-dropping animal sightings, cultural experiences that will extend your horizons and memories that will last a lifetime.*

Chapter 2: When to Visit and What to Bring

Are you planning your Ugandan and Rwandan adventure? Choosing when to come and what to bring in your trusty bag are critical initial steps. Fear not, intrepid traveler, for this chapter has all you need to know about navigating the seasons and packing like a pro!

2.1 Best Time to Visit Uganda: The Land of Eternal Spring

Uganda has a lovely climate all year round, however, there are small seasonal fluctuations to consider. Overall, the nation has two rainy seasons (March-May and September-November) and two dry seasons (December-February and June-August). Let's break down what this implies for your trip:

Dry Season Delights (December-February and June-August):
Wildlife Watching at Its Best: Sunshine makes creatures happy! Dry savannas make viewing animals simpler, and gorilla trekking permits are more widely accessible during these times.

Imagine amazing encounters with gorgeous lions, elegant giraffes, and, of course, awe-inspiring gorillas.
Unobstructed Skies and Stunning Sunsets: Dry skies provide unobstructed vistas, ideal for photographing landscapes and animals. And don't miss the flaming sunsets that will paint the horizon in bright colors.

Pleasant Temperatures: The dry season provides ideal temperatures that are neither too hot nor too humid, making exploring more pleasurable. Think breezy mornings, pleasant afternoons, and cold nights - ideal for layering garments.
Peak Season Crowds: Dry season popularity comes with a cost, including somewhat higher costs and probably greater crowds at famous tourist destinations. Book your gorilla permits and lodgings well in advance, particularly during high holiday seasons.

Wet Season Wonders (March-May; September-November):
Emerald Everything: During the rainy season, Uganda becomes a lush green. The waterfalls grow even more beautiful, and the environment takes on a mysterious, even primordial quality. Consider magnificent jungles bursting with life and flowing waterfalls plummeting into green valleys.

Fewer Crowds and (Sometimes) reduced Prices: The rainy season provides a more peaceful tourist experience with perhaps reduced lodging costs. So, if you want a more personal exploration, this may be the ideal site for you.

Embrace the Adventure: Be prepared for the odd rain shower. Pack a decent raincoat and waterproof footwear, and keep in mind that the roads may be slick. However, a little rain never hurts an expedition, right?

Bonus Tip: Shoulder seasons (between dry and rainy) might provide an excellent blend of pleasant temperatures and fewer visitors.

2.2 Best Time to Visit Rwanda: The Land of a Thousand Hills and Diverse Delights.

Rwanda, like Uganda, has a moderate temperature throughout the year, with two rainy and two dry seasons. Here's a breakdown to help you choose:

Dry Season Delights (December-February and June-August):

Prime Time for Gorilla Trekking and Wildlife Watching: Similar to Uganda, the dry season delivers a clear sky, making gorilla trekking and wildlife watching more enjoyable.

Consider spectacular encounters with mountain gorillas in the volcanic scenery and exhilarating safaris in Akagera National Park.

Hiking Bliss: Dry pathways make it easy to explore beautiful places like Volcanoes National Park. Imagine yourself ascending volcanic hills and taking in stunning panoramic vistas.

Pleasant temps: Similar to Uganda, the dry season provides moderate temps for exploration without breaking a sweat.

Peak Season visitors: Popular attractions during the dry season may see higher prices and bigger visitors. Book your gorilla permits and lodgings well in advance, particularly during high holiday seasons.

Wet Season Wonders (March-May; September-November):
Lush Landscapes and Fewer Crowds: Rwanda's natural splendor reaches its zenith during the rainy season. Waterfalls scream, wildflowers flourish, and the air is crisp. There may also be fewer crowds, which might result in reduced lodging costs.

Embrace the Adventure: Bring a raincoat and be prepared for the odd rainstorm. Consider the possibility of slick roads while making your trip arrangements.

Bonus Tip: The shoulder seasons provide an excellent blend of moderate temperatures and maybe fewer visitors.

2.3 Packing Essentials for Uganda & Rwanda: Ready for Adventure

Now that you know when to go, let's talk about packing like a pro explorer! Here's a list of necessities for your Uganda and Rwanda adventure:

Clothing:

Layers: Temperatures fluctuate according to height and time of day. Pack lightweight, breathable layers that may be easily mixed and matched.

Quick-drying clothing is a lifesaver, particularly during the rainy season or after strenuous activities. Choose moisture-wicking textiles such as polyester or merino wool.

Long-sleeved shirts and pants are needed for sun protection, bug bites, and sudden temperature reductions at higher elevations.

Convertible Hiking trousers: These trousers zip off into shorts, making them suitable for a variety of activities and weather situations.

Rain Gear: A high-quality rain jacket and waterproof leggings are essential, particularly during the rainy season.

Durable Hiking Boots: With uneven terrain and the possibility of rain showers, durable, comfortable hiking boots with adequate ankle support are essential.

Essentials:

Sunglasses and a sun hat are essential for protecting oneself from the harsh African sun. To provide maximum coverage, use a wide-brimmed hat and polarized sunglasses.

Reusable Water Bottle: Staying hydrated is essential, particularly during hot weather. Consider using a reusable water bottle with a filter to reduce plastic waste.

Headlamp or Flashlight: Power shortages might occur, and exploring at night may need a dependable light source.

Pack a simple first-aid kit with bandages, antiseptic wipes, and pain medications for small cuts, scrapes, and headaches.

Personal Toiletries: Bring your typical toiletries, but choose eco-friendly products like biodegradable sunscreen and shampoo bars to reduce your environmental effects.

Optional but useful:
Binoculars: A decent set of binoculars can help you see animals better.

Camera and extra batteries: Capture all of your fantastic experiences! Pack additional batteries and a memory card with ample space.

Insect Repellent: A good insect repellent, particularly one containing DEET, will help keep annoying mosquitos away.

Stay connected with a global power adaptor that is compatible with Rwandan and Ugandan outlets.

Remember:
- Before packing, check the airline's luggage limitations.
- Consider the washing facilities at your lodgings; packing light enables you to simply wash and reuse garments.
- Respect local cultures by dressing modestly, particularly while visiting religious places.

Chapter 3: Visas and Permits: Unlocking the Gates of Adventure (Without the Headache)

Alright, adventurer. Before you board an aircraft and escape reality for the wilds of Uganda and Rwanda, there are a few bureaucratic hurdles to clear. Fear not, since this chapter will guide you through the process of obtaining visas and permits, which are the first steps toward your epic African journey!

3.1 Visa Requirements for Uganda: The Pearl of Africa is Awaiting!

Good news! Most nations may get a visa to Uganda upon arrival at Entebbe International Airport or other major border crossing. Here is the lowdown:

- Visa Type: East African Tourist Visa (valid in Uganda, Rwanda, and Kenya).
- Cost: USD 50 (subject to vary; double-check before flying)
- Validity: A single entry is valid for thirty days.

What You'll Need: A passport (valid for at least 6 months after your trip dates), a completed visa application form (typically accessible at the airport), and evidence of adequate finances (bank statement or credit card).

Bonus Tip: Save time by completing the visa application form online before your trip: https://visas.immigration.go.ug/.

Feeling fancy? If you want to remain for more than 30 days, you may apply for a multiple-entry visa in advance at a Ugandan embassy or consulate in your home country.

Always check with the Ugandan embassy or consulate in your home country for the most current visa information and any possible changes in requirements.

3.2 Visa Requirements in Rwanda: The Land of a Thousand Hills Welcomes You

Like Uganda, most nations may get a visa for Rwanda upon arrival at Kigali International Airport or other major border crossing. Here's a breakdown:

Tourist Visa

- Cost: USD 30 (subject to vary; double-check before flying).
- Validity: A single entry is valid for thirty days.

What You'll Need: Your passport (valid for at least six months after your trip dates), a completed visa application form (typically accessible at the airport), and evidence of onward travel (flight confirmation or bus ticket).

- Bonus Tip: Similar to Uganda, Rwanda enables you to fill out the visa application form online before your trip: https://support.irembo.gov.rw/en/support/solutions/folders/47000777837

Feeling fancy? Similar to Uganda, multiple-entry visas are available for lengthier visits and may be sought in advance from a Rwandan embassy or consulate in your home country.

Heads Up: Before your journey, double-check the most recent visa information with the Rwandan embassy or consulate in your home country, just like you would with Uganda.

3.3 Getting Gorilla Trekking Permits: Face-to-Face with Gentle Giants (But Remember the Permit!)

Now, let's speak about the golden ticket to an extraordinary experience: the gorilla trekking permit! These permits are very restricted to protect the gorillas, therefore scheduling in advance is critical. Here's how to get yours:

Booking with a Licensed Tour Operator: This is the most convenient choice. They will manage all of the paperwork and logistics for you, resulting in a stress-free experience.

Book Directly Through the Ugandan Wildlife Authority (UWA) or Rwanda Development Board (RDB): Budget-conscious adventurers may book permits online through the relevant government websites (links below). However, be prepared to do some additional effort and compete for permits, particularly during high season.

Costs and Websites:

Uganda charges USD 700 per person. Permits may be booked online via the Uganda Wildlife Authority (UWA) at https://ugandawildlife.org/

Rwanda: US$1,500 per person. Permits may be booked online via the Rwanda Development Board (RDB) at https://visitrwandabookings.rdb.rw/rdbportal/mountain-gorilla-tracking

Planning is essential: Gorilla trekking permits sometimes sell out months in advance, particularly during peak season. Book your permits as soon as your trip dates are known to prevent disappointment.

Important Note: Gorilla hiking demands average fitness. Check with your doctor beforehand to confirm you're physically capable of handling difficult terrain at higher elevations.

Remember: responsible tourism is essential! Respect the gorillas and their environment by adhering to your guide's advice and keeping a safe distance from these majestic animals.

Chapter 4: Getting There and Getting Around: Conquering the Sky and Hitting the Road (Without Getting Lost)

Okay, intrepid adventurer! So you've arranged for your visas, obtained your gorilla trekking permit (if required), and your suitcases are virtually bursting with excitement. Now comes the exciting part: going to Uganda and Rwanda! This chapter will help you navigate airports, choose the best form of transportation, and arrive safely in the heart of Africa.

4.1 Flights to Uganda and Rwanda: Soaring Like an Eagle (Without Feathered Wings)

There are no direct flights to Uganda or Rwanda from most major US cities. Fear not, fellow adventurer! There are several connecting flights available to bring you to your East African trip.

Here is the lowdown:

Major Airlines: Ethiopian Airlines, Kenya Airways, RwandAir, Qatar Airways, and Emirates provide connecting flights to Entebbe International Airport (Uganda) and Kigali International Airport (Rwanda).

Flight Time: Flight timings might vary from 18 to 24 hours, depending on your starting point and number of connections.

Cost: Flight rates might vary based on the airline, the season, and how far ahead you book. A roundtrip ticket from the United States typically costs between USD 1,000 and USD 3,000.

- Pro tip: Be a wise traveler! Use travel comparison websites and apps to locate the greatest flight bargains. Consider flying into one country and out of another to create a more flexible itinerary.

Once you land:
- Entebbe and Kigali airports are both small and simple to traverse. English is commonly spoken, so navigating should be simple.
- Visas on Arrival: As indicated in Chapter 3, Uganda and Rwanda both provide visas on arrival to most nations. Follow the visible signs and have your documentation ready for a seamless transaction.
- Currency Exchange: Both airports provide currency exchange booths, however, the prices may not be competitive. Consider exchanging a modest amount for your first costs and then

visiting a local bank or ATM for higher rates once you're in town.

Bonus Tip: Before you arrive, get a dependable offline map app for your phone. This will come in handy if you ever get lost or don't have access to the Internet.

4.2 Transportation Options in Uganda: Driving Ugandan-Style

Now that you've landed, it's time to explore! Here's an overview of your transportation choices in Uganda:

- Domestic flights, although not the most cost-effective alternative, may save you time when traveling great distances, especially if you're short on time. Several small airlines fly between major cities, including Entebbe, Kasese (for gorilla trekking), and Mburo National Park.

- Matatus: These brilliantly colored minibusses form the backbone of Uganda's public transportation. They're an inexpensive and exciting way to travel but be prepared for congested circumstances and possibly lengthy trip durations.

- Taxis: Taxis are widely accessible in big cities like Kampala. To minimize surprises, agree on a fee before you get in.

- Car rentals provide the greatest freedom, particularly if you want to visit off-the-beaten-path sites. Just be aware that traffic conditions might change, and driving in Kampala can be confusing for the untrained. An international driver's license is necessary.

Pro Tip: If you're feeling brave and know how to negotiate, try renting a boda boda (motorcycle taxi). This is an exciting (and even dangerous) way to get about, but it's not for the faint of heart!

4.3 Transportation Options in Rwanda: Exploring Rwanda by Wheels

Similar to Uganda, Rwanda has a range of transportation alternatives to fit your budget and travel style:

Domestic Flights: Rwanda Air provides limited domestic flights inside the country, principally linking Kigali to places near national parks such as Akagera and Volcanos.

Shared minibusses provide a pleasant and cost-effective option to travel between Rwanda's main cities. They are often less packed than Ugandan matatus and provide a more relaxing journey.

Taxis: Taxis are widely accessible in Kigali and other large cities. Metered taxis are becoming increasingly prevalent, but if the taxi does not have a meter, agree on a fee ahead of time.

Car rentals give you the greatest flexibility to explore Rwanda at your leisure. Rwanda's roads are typically in decent condition when compared to neighboring nations. An international driver's license is necessary, the same as it is in Uganda.

Rwanda is a tiny nation, so traveling by bicycle is an excellent choice for the athletic visitor. Several tour providers offer bike trips across gorgeous landscapes, enabling you to genuinely interact with Rwanda's countryside.

Bonus Tip: If you're feeling sociable and want to get a real sense of Rwandan life, take a "moto" (motorcycle taxi). It's an inexpensive and effective way to get about, but remember to wear a helmet for safety!

Remember:

No matter the mode of transportation you select, stay patient and enjoy the journey! Traffic in Kigali may be crowded at peak hours, and unexpected delays are part of the adventure of visiting Africa. So sit back, relax, and take in the sights and sounds around you.

With this chapter completed, you are well on your way to conquering the skies and traversing the streets of Uganda and Rwanda.

Chapter 5: Health & Safety: Keep You Adventuring Worry-Free (Without the Drama)

Okay, intrepid explorer! You've prepared for the travel, you've arranged for transportation, and you're undoubtedly filled with anticipation. But, before you venture into the wilds of Uganda and Rwanda, let's speak about being healthy and safe. This chapter provides important vaccines, travel insurance suggestions, and a few practical hints to ensure a smooth and worry-free journey.

5.1 Recommended Vaccinations for Uganda and Rwanda: Staying Healthy (and Adventure-Ready)

Vaccinations are essential for safeguarding oneself against avoidable illnesses when traveling. Here's a breakdown of the recommended immunizations in

Uganda and Rwanda:

Yellow fever vaccine is required for entrance to both Uganda and Rwanda. Make sure your yellow fever vaccination certificate is stamped and signed by a registered physician, since you may need it to show immigration authorities upon arrival.

Highly recommended.

Measles, Mumps, and Rubella (MMR): This is recommended for all travelers, regardless of location.

Hepatitis A and B vaccinations protect against liver illnesses caused by contaminated food or water.

Typhoid: This vaccination protects against a dangerous bacterial illness transmitted by contaminated food or water.

Rabies: This vaccination is advised for tourists who go off the beaten path or participate in activities that enhance their risk of animal bites.

Additional considerations:

Meningitis immunization may be suggested based on the duration of your stay and the activities you intend to do. Consult your doctor to determine your unique risk.

Malaria is found in some areas of Uganda and Rwanda. Consult your doctor about malaria prophylactic medicine to avoid infection.

Remember, this is just a rough guideline. The particular immunizations you'll need will be determined by your health, itinerary, and activities. Always visit a travel medicine professional or your doctor at least 8 weeks before your trip to discuss your requirements and verify you're up to date on any necessary vaccines.

5.2 Travel Insurance Considerations: Peace of Mind for the Unexpected.

Travel insurance provides peace of mind. It may help you avoid unforeseen financial constraints in the event of vacation cancellations, medical problems, or misplaced baggage. Here are things to think about when selecting travel insurance for your Uganda and

Rwanda adventure:
Medical Coverage: Make sure your insurance covers medical expenditures overseas, such as hospitalization and emergency evacuation. Consider the appropriate amount of coverage depending on your activity and health risks.

Vacation Cancellation/Interruption: Choose coverage that protects you against financial damages if you must cancel your vacation due to unexpected reasons, such as sickness or natural catastrophes.

Baggage and Personal possessions: Get protection against lost, stolen, or damaged baggage and possessions.

Pro Tip: Compare several travel insurance policies to pick one that provides the coverage you want at a reasonable cost. Read the tiny print carefully to see what is included and excluded from the policy.

Bonus Tip: Look for travel insurance that includes adventurous activities such as gorilla trekking. Not all plans do, so be sure you're fully covered if you want to go on any exciting adventures.

By following these guidelines and taking the appropriate measures, you may have a healthy and safe experience in Uganda and Rwanda. Let us now explore the interesting world of lodging possibilities, which range from opulent lodges buried in stunning surroundings to low-cost campgrounds beneath a starry sky!

Chapter 6: Money Matters: Making Your Ugandan Shillings Stretch Further Than a Yogi (Without Breaking the Bank)

So you've taken care of your health, you've purchased travel insurance, and all that remains is to work out the "money" issue. Don't worry, this chapter will help you navigate Ugandan shillings and Rwandan francs, which are the lifeblood of your East African expedition.

6.1 Currency Exchange in Uganda and Rwanda: Don't Be a "Mzungu" with Money Problems ("Mzungu" is a Kiswahili name for foreigner)

Uganda and Rwanda's official currencies are the Ugandan Shilling (UGX) and Rwandan Franc (RWF), respectively. While this seems like something out of a fantasy story, converting your hard-earned cash is pretty simple.

41

Exchange Your Benjamins (or Euros) for Local Currency:

Airports: Both Entebbe and Kigali airports feature currency exchange facilities, albeit the prices may not be the greatest. Consider exchanging a modest amount to cover early expenditures such as cabs and refreshments.

Banks and ATMs are widely accessible in major cities and tourist destinations. Using your debit card to withdraw local cash is typically the easiest and most cost-effective method. Just be careful of any withdrawal fees that your bank may impose.

Bureau de Change: These money exchange booths are common in most towns and cities. Before converting money, shop around to get the best rates. Always inquire about any hidden costs or charges.

- Pro tip: Don't carry too much cash around. ATMs are your buddy, and credit cards are accepted at most places in popular tourist destinations.

- *Insider Tip:* While Uganda and Rwanda are moving toward cashless transactions, certain smaller establishments and rural regions may still prefer cash. Keeping a small amount of local cash on hand is usually a smart idea.

6.2 Budgeting Tips for Your Trip: Ballin' on a Budget (Without Feeling Like a Cheapskate).

Let's face it: travel may be pricey! But do not worry, budget-conscious explorer! Here are a few suggestions to help you stretch your Ugandan shillings and Rwandan francs further:

Accommodation options include anything from upscale lodges to budget-friendly hostels and campgrounds. Research your alternatives and choose something that complements your style and budget.

Transportation: Matatus (Uganda) and shared minibuses (Rwanda) are inexpensive and exciting ways to move about. Taxis might be more costly, so negotiate a price in advance.

Food: Enjoy the local food! Street food booths provide excellent and economical lunches. Don't be hesitant to try something new; you could find your new favorite meal!

While gorilla climbing is an expensive activity, there are lots of free or low-cost alternatives, such as exploring local markets, hiking through breathtaking landscapes, and visiting cultural sites.

Bargaining is a common practice across Africa. Do not be scared to bargain at souvenir markets or with taxi drivers (but be courteous and have fun!).

Bonus Tip: Travel during the shoulder seasons (between peak and dry seasons) to perhaps get better bargains on flights and accommodations.

Remember, you don't have to break the bank to have an unforgettable trip in Uganda and Rwanda. By following these guidelines and being a little resourceful, you may enjoy all these great nations have to offer without feeling like a "Mzungu" with no money!

Chapter 7: Language and Culture: Bridging the Gap (Without Any Faux Pas).

Okay, world adventurer! You have your funds in order, your bag is almost ready, and excitement is undoubtedly coursing through your veins. But, before you fly out on your Ugandan and Rwandan journey, let's talk about language and culture, which are the keys to a genuinely rewarding experience. This chapter provides you with key terminology, cultural conventions, and personal experiences to help you avoid embarrassing mistakes and traverse these great nations with confidence and respect.

7.1 Essential Phrases in English, Luganda (Uganda), and Kinyarwanda.

While English is spoken in certain tourist destinations, learning a few simple words in the native languages of Luganda (Uganda) and Kinyarwanda (Rwanda) may go a long way. It demonstrates respect for the culture and may lead to more real relationships with locals.

Here are a few useful phrases to get you started:
Hello:
English: Hello

Luganda: Mwe Bana (informal) / Mu'ssebo (formal)
Kinyarwanda: Muraho

Thank you:
English: Thank you
Luganda: Webale Nnyo
Kinyarwanda: Murakoze cyane

Please:
English: Please
Luganda: Njagala (pronounced N-jah-ga-la)
Kinyarwanda: Ndakwingira

Yes:
English: Yes
Luganda: Ye
Kinyarwanda: Yego

No:
English: No
Luganda: Nedda
Kinyarwanda: Oya

Bonus Phrase:
How much is this?
English: How much is this?
Luganda: Eno Erindi (pronounced E-no Eh-rin-di)
Kinyarwanda: Ibi ni birame ese? (pronounced ee-bee nee bee-rah-may eh-seh)

Pro tip: Download an excellent offline translation program on your phone. It may be quite useful when you need to translate anything quickly.

7.2 Understanding Ugandan and Rwandan Culture: A Crash Course (With a Personal Story About a Goat)

Uganda and Rwanda have vibrant civilizations rich in heritage. Understanding a few fundamental rules can help you have a positive and courteous experience.

Here are a few things to remember:
- Handshakes are the most prevalent form of greeting. In Rwanda, it is usual to give a small bow as a token of respect, particularly when meeting elders.

- While there is no official clothing requirement, it is usually advisable to dress modestly, particularly while visiting religious places. Avoid too exposing apparel or anything with objectionable messages.
- Bargaining is common in marketplaces and with taxi drivers. Be nice, have fun, and don't be afraid to walk away if you don't obtain a price you agree with.

47

- Cultural Shock Confession: Speaking of cultural faux pas, let me share a humorous incident from my first trip to Uganda. I was visiting a small town and, to be pleasant, stroked a random goat on the head. It turned out the goat belonged to the local leader, and it didn't like visitors patting its head! Needless to say, there was some bewilderment (and amusement) before I humbly (no pun intended) apologized for my cultural inexperience.

Lesson learned: a little cultural awareness goes a long way!

Remember to embrace diversity! Cultural contacts are what make travel so fulfilling. Be courteous, ask questions if you are unclear, and have an open mind. This will allow you to develop a greater respect for Ugandan and Rwandan culture while also creating experiences that will last a lifetime.

Part 2:

Exploring Uganda

Chapter 8: Kampala: The beautiful capital of Uganda

Strap on, explorers, because we're diving into Uganda's exciting capital, Kampala! This vibrant metropolis is a beating heart, bringing life and culture to the whole nation. Prepare for busy marketplaces brimming with colorful wares, ancient sites whispering stories of bygone kingdoms, and a vibrant nightlife scene beneath Uganda's starry sky. Kampala is a city that will tempt your taste buds with superb local food, test your negotiating abilities at bustling marketplaces, and take your breath away with its surprising beauty. So saddle up, because Chapter 8 is your one-stop guide to conquering Kampala!

8.1 Must-See Sights in Kampala: A Sensory Delight for the Adventurous Soul

Kampala is a delightful variety of sights, sounds, and experiences for all types of adventurers. Here are a few must-see attractions to fill your itinerary:

The Uganda Museum will immerse you in Uganda's rich history and cultural tapestry. This intriguing museum has a remarkable collection of items, including antique weapons and traditional musical instruments. Expect to be transported across time as you tour exhibitions illustrating the rise and fall of kingdoms, tribal customs, and the history of Ugandan art.

Kasubi Tombs: Visit the slopes of Kasubi Hill and learn about the intriguing Buganda Kingdom's history. The Kasubi Tombs, the customary burial site of Buganda rulers, are classified as a UNESCO World Heritage site. These architectural wonders are embellished with delicate strawwork and have a long history; just remember to dress modestly as a gesture of respect.

Namirembe church: For architectural beauty, visit Namirembe Cathedral, an Anglican church that towers above the city. Its unusual red-brick exterior and Gothic Revival architecture provide a striking contrast to the busy streets underneath. Take a minute to appreciate the stained-glass windows and enjoy the serene atmosphere inside the cathedral walls.

Baha'i House of Worship: This architectural marvel, known as the "Mashariki Temple," is a breathtaking example of Baha'i architecture. Its nine-sided form and detailed decorations are stunning, and the peaceful environment within encourages introspection and thought.

Old Kampala Hill: History aficionados, this is for you! Kampala's birthplace, Old Kampala Hill, is home to historical buildings such as the Uganda National Mosque and Parliament Buildings. Wander around the small streets, take in the local ambiance, and visualize the city's transformation from a collection of huts to a booming metropolis.

Bonus Tip: If you're feeling brave (and have a strong stomach), visit the Nakasero Market, a maze of booths filled with everything conceivable. Prepare yourself for sensory overload; the sights, scents, and sounds are all unique experiences! Just remember to negotiate with a smile and show respect to the dealers.

During my visit to Nakasero Market, I got lost for an hour (or two) in the colorful mayhem. But instead of worrying, I chose to appreciate the experience. I ended up conversing with a lovely trader who showed me how to haggle for the best Ugandan coffee beans (and let me just say, my negotiating abilities increased dramatically!).

Getting lost may lead to the most unexpected and gratifying experiences!

This is just a sample of what Kampala has to offer. Prepare to be fascinated by the city's contagious energy as you explore secret passageways and find one-of-a-kind street art. Remember that the genuine beauty of Kampala is not just in its scenery, but also in its people. Strike up a conversation with a local, try some wonderful street cuisine, and let yourself get carried away by the vivid energy of this incredible city.

8.2 Cultural Experiences in Kampala: Introducing the Ugandan Soul

Move over, museums, because, in this chapter, we're leaving the typical tourist track and delving deep into Kampala's lively cultural undercurrent! Forget cookie-cutter experiences; here's your opportunity to connect with the Ugandan spirit and make memories that will last long after you leave.

1. *Witness the Power of Storytelling at the Ndere Cultural Centre.*

This bustling cultural institution is a treasure mine of Ugandan heritage. Immerse yourself in a spectacular performance including the various dances, music, and traditions of Uganda's many ethnic groups. From the lively Baganda dances to the mournful music of the Acholi people, expect to be captivated by the raw talent and rich cultural tapestry on show. It's more than simply a performance; it's a trip through Uganda's heart and soul.

2. Explore the Buzzing Batwa Community: (Be aware that some travelers may find portions of these trips unethical.)
While not officially in Kampala, a visit to a Batwa pygmy settlement near the city provides insight into a distinct and intriguing way of life. For millennia, the Batwa people lived as hunter-gatherers in Central Africa's woods. Conservation initiatives have resulted in the displacement of numerous Batwa villages. Former Batwa inhabitants provide ethical tours that teach visitors about their traditional way of life, hardships, and prospects. Make sure you select a tour operator that values responsible tourism and cultural sensitivity.

3. Explore the artistic heart of Uganda at a local art gallery:
Kampala has a bustling art culture, and what better way to enjoy it than to visit local galleries? Immerse

yourself in the vivid colors, detailed sculptures, and thought-provoking artworks that depict Ugandans and their views on the world. You could even come upon a one-of-a-kind piece of art to take home as a keepsake from your vacation. (Pro tip: Haggling is allowed at many art galleries, so put your negotiating talents to the test!)

4. Learn the art of Ugandan cooking with a local family:
Food is a global language, and what better way to learn about Ugandan culture than by cooking a traditional dinner with a local family? Many tour companies include cooking workshops where you can discover the secrets of Ugandan classics such as matoke (steamed

55

green bananas), Rolex (a Ugandan chapati stuffed with different toppings), and flavorful stews. Not only will you learn to cook, but you will also get to know Ugandan hospitality and make memorable experiences in a warm and friendly setting.

5. *Catch a local band and let the rhythm take over.*
Kampala's nightlife is famed, and what better way to experience the city's colorful atmosphere than to see a local band? From throbbing Afrobeat rhythms to beautiful ballads, Kampala's music culture has something for everyone. Grab a nice Ugandan beer (Bell Lager, anyone?) and interact with the welcoming people as the contagious energy of Ugandan music washes over you. You could just find your new favorite band and dance the night away beneath the starry Ugandan sky.

Bonus Tip: Don't be scared to leave your comfort zone! Strike up a discussion with locals in a crowded market, attend a traditional ritual (if asked), or just stroll through a neighborhood park and absorb up Ugandans' daily lives. These unexpected interactions are frequently the most enjoyable aspects of traveling.

Chapter 9: Bwindi Impenetrable National Park: Tracking Gentle Giants (Without Annoying Them)

Alright, adrenaline seekers! We've visited the electrified pulse of Kampala, and now it's time to journey into Uganda's green heart, Bwindi Impenetrable National Park. This UNESCO World Heritage Site is a foggy refuge steeped in mystery, home to majestic mountain gorillas. Consider this scenario: you're carving your way through lush jungles, sunshine dappling the forest floor when you come face to face with a silverback gorilla, a beast of enormous might and remarkable tenderness. Yes, my friends, gorilla trekking is going to be your new passion!

But, before you pack your khaki safari outfit (which may make for some spectacular Instagram photos), let's get into the details of gorilla trekking in Bwindi. This chapter provides you with all of the necessary information, from obtaining your golden gorilla permit to acting like a responsible visitor amid these beautiful animals.

9.1 Gorilla Trekking Permits and Booking Information: Don't Be Shut Out (by a Gorilla or Park Ranger)

Here's the deal: gorilla permits are quite valuable in Uganda. The number of tourists permitted to witness these gentle giants is tightly controlled to safeguard the gorillas and their environment. So it's critical to plan and book ahead of time.

Permit Prices: Be prepared to spend some money. Gorilla trekking permits are not inexpensive, but this is a once-in-a-lifetime opportunity, right? Prices may vary but expect to spend roughly $700 for a permit.

Booking Channels: You cannot just go up to Bwindi and expect to see gorillas. Permits are regulated by the Uganda Wildlife Authority (UWA), therefore book directly with them or a trustworthy travel operator.

Don't fall for sketchy web offers; believe me, seeing a cranky park ranger isn't part of the fun.

Planning: Because permits are limited, particularly during peak season (June to August and December to February), it is strongly advised to arrange your gorilla trek months, if not years, in advance. In this instance, the early bird gets the gorilla!

Pro Tip 1: Combine your gorilla hike with a visit to Rwanda's Volcanoes National Park. Both provide great gorilla encounters, yet permit availability may differ between the two parks.

Pro Tip 2: There are many habituated gorilla families in Bwindi, each with their distinct characteristics. If you have a choice (for example, whether you want to see lively kids or a stately silverback), inform your tour operator when you book. They may be able to advise you on the ideal gorilla family trip for your preferences.

9.2 What to Expect on a Gorilla Trek: Prepare for Adventure (and Perhaps a Little Mud).

Trekking gorillas is no easy task (pun intended). Bwindi is a genuine jungle, and the terrain may be difficult. Here's what you may expect:

Prepare for an early wake-up call. Treks usually begin before daybreak, so bring your spirit of adventure and a strong cup of Ugandan coffee (believe me, you'll need it).

Trekking Through the Jungle: Rainforest pathways may be muddy, slippery, and occasionally quite steep. Think Indiana Jones but with fewer snakes and many more gorillas (hopefully). Hiking footwear with strong ankle support is essential!

The real journey time varies depending on where the gorilla family is situated. But when you eventually meet these gorgeous animals, it will all be worthwhile. Just remember that you're in their land, so respect it and heed your guide's advice. (No gorilla selfies, please!)

The Magical Hour: You will only get one magical hour to view gorillas in their natural environment. Observe cheerful children playing in the bush, a silverback eating contentedly on leaves, or a mother gently cuddling her infant. It's an experience you'll never forget.

Bonus Tip: Bring some food and water for the hike. Hiking through a jungle may be unexpectedly energy-draining, so remain hydrated. Just be sure to dispose of your waste appropriately, leaving no trace behind!

Gorilla Etiquette 101: These gentle giants have earned our respect. Here are a few golden guidelines to remember:

- Maintain a distance of at least 7 meters (23 feet) from the gorillas at all times. This protects them from infections spread by humans.

- Silence is golden: Avoid loud sounds and quick movements. The gorillas are quickly startled, and you want a calm interaction, correct?

- No flash photography: Flash might disturb gorillas' normal behavior. Use standard camera settings and zoom in for spectacular gorilla selfies (from a safe distance, of course!).

- Keep it clean by disposing of your tissues and other garbage correctly. Remember, you are a visitor in their house, so leave it as clean as you found it.

- No looking down at the silverback: A silverback gorilla may interpret direct eye contact as a challenge. If a silverback establishes eye contact with you, move away gently and politely. Don't worry; your guide will know how to manage the issue (and don't attempt to exert power - you'll lose).

Following these basic instructions will result in a safe and courteous interaction for both you and the gorillas. Remember that ethical tourism is critical to the protection of these wonderful species.

9.3 Responsible Gorilla Trekking Practices: Be a Force of Good (Not a Banana-Tossing Tourist)

Gorilla trekking is a privilege, yet with it comes responsibility. Here's how you can use your journey through Bwindi to make a difference:

Choose Responsible Tour Operators: Conduct research and arrange your trip with a reputed tour operator who values gorilla care and sustainable methods. Look for businesses that assist local communities and environmental initiatives.

Respect the Habitat: Stay on authorized routes to prevent damaging the sensitive rainforest ecology. Leave no trace by packing away all of your waste and avoiding using any dangerous chemicals around the gorillas, such as DEET-containing bug repellents.

Consider giving to groups committed to gorilla conservation. Your donation contributes to the long-term survival of these amazing monkeys.

By adopting these ethical practices, you can help guarantee that future generations can enjoy the enchantment of seeing mountain gorillas in their natural environment. Remember that it's not just about crossing something off your bucket list; it's about having a good influence on the world around you.

So, are you prepared to go on this incredible adventure? Using the knowledge in this chapter, you'll be well on your way to monitoring gorillas in Bwindi Impenetrable National Park. Just bring your spirit of adventure and a healthy respect for these gentle giants, and prepare for an encounter that will transform the way you view the world.

Chapter 10: Queen Elizabeth National Park: Where Wildlife Roams Free (And Might Steal Your Breakfast)

Buckle up, nature aficionados! Chapter 10 transports you to the heart of Queen Elizabeth National Park, a vast grassland filled with wildlife. Imagine you're driving through the golden meadows in a safari vehicle, seeing a pride of lions resting in the morning light or a stately elephant silhouetted against a flaming sunset. Queen Elizabeth National Park provides a wildlife show like no other, with encounters that will leave you breathless.

10.1 Wildlife Viewing in Queen Elizabeth National Park: Spotting Everything From Lions to Tree-Climbing Lions.

Queen Elizabeth National Park has a remarkable range of animals, making it a safari hotspot. Here's a look at the stars of the show:

Big Cats: Lions, leopards, and cheetahs live in the park. Keep a watch out for these gorgeous predators hunting their prey or reclining magnificently among the long grasses.

Elephants: These gentle giants are often seen at Queen Elizabeth. Witness them grazing calmly, trumpeting sounds resounding over the savanna, or even (get ready) a rare encounter with tree-climbing lions - yep, you read it correctly! Queen Elizabeth is home to a unique population of lions that have adapted to reclining in the acacia trees, providing some stunning views.

Primates: Look for lively chimps swinging through the trees in Kyambura Gorge, as well as elusive habituated black and white colobus monkeys.

Buffalo Herds: Witness the thunderous strength of a buffalo herd as it stampedes over the plains, a sight that is both awe-inspiring and scary (in a good way!).

And the list goes on: the park is home to more than 600 bird species, including the stately crowned crane and the secretive shoebill stork. Keep a look out for antelopes, zebras, warthogs, and a variety of other wonderful animals.

Pro Tip 1: The best times to watch the game are early in the morning and late in the afternoon. The animals are more active during these chilly hours, which increases your chances of seeing them.

Pro Tip 2: Hire a reliable safari guide. Their understanding of the area and animal behavior will greatly improve your safari experience. They'll know where to go for the greatest sightings and can answer any questions you have about animals.

10.2 Kazinga Channel Boat Cruise: A Hippo Haven with Unexpected Encounters

Queen Elizabeth National Park provides more than simply thrilling wildlife drives. Take a picturesque boat tour along the Kazinga Channel, a 40-kilometer canal that connects Lake Edward and Lake George. This peaceful stretch of water is a sanctuary for animals and provides a unique view of the park's environment.

Here is what awaiting you:

Hippo Heaven: Prepare for a cute (if somewhat disturbing) overdose of hippos! The Kazinga Channel has one of the greatest hippopotamus densities in Africa. Witness these massive beasts reclining in the sun, snorting hello, or just relaxing in the water - but don't go too near; these guys are territorial!

Crocodile Encounters: Keep an eye out for the odd Nile crocodile hiding in the murky water. These ancient creatures offer excitement to your boat journey. The Kazinga Channel is an avian paradise. Look for colorful kingfishers, magnificent African fish eagles, and a variety of other feathered companions.

Unexpected Delights: You never know what you'll find on your boat tour. Elephants are known to come down to the water's edge for a drink, while buffalo and other animals are often seen cooling down in the channel.

Bonus Tip: Boat trips normally run around two hours. Remember to bring sunscreen, a hat, and a camera - you'll want to preserve these wonderful moments!

10.3 Accommodation Options Near Queen Elizabeth National Park: Relaxing After a Day of Wildlife Encounters.

After a wonderful day of visiting the park, you'll need a comfy spot to lay your tired head. Queen Elizabeth National Park has a wide range of housing alternatives to suit every budget and style:

Luxury lodges:

Mweya Safari Resort: This sumptuous resort, nestled on the banks of the Kazinga Channel, provides breathtaking vistas, exquisite facilities, and exceptional service. Expect infinity pools and excellent food

Ishasha Wilderness Camp: This deluxe tented camp, nestled in the park's Ishasha region, is known for its tree-climbing lions and provides a one-of-a-kind and spectacular experience. Imagine falling asleep to the sounds of the African wilderness and waking up to see a lion resting in an acacia tree nearby! (Expect costs of approximately $300 per night.)

Mid-range lodges:

Mburo Green Haven resort: This eco-friendly resort provides comfortable lodgings, great meals, and the opportunity to enjoy the splendor of the park without breaking the budget. (Prices normally vary between $150 and $250 each night.)

Katunguru Bush Lodge offers a rustic but pleasant environment inside the park. Relax on your balcony, taking in the views and sounds of the African environment. (Expect rates between $100 and $200 per night.)

Budget-Friendly Options:
Uganda Wildlife Authority Camps: The Uganda Wildlife Authority (UWA) manages many modest campsites around the park. These provide a straightforward camping experience, enabling you to get up close and personal with nature. (Camping costs are normally quite reasonable, at $20-30 per night.)

Homestays: Several small settlements around the park provide homestay possibilities. This is an excellent approach to immerse oneself in Ugandan culture and the local way of life. (Prices vary based on the homestay, but they are often the most affordable choice.)

Choosing the Right Accommodation:
When choosing an accommodation, keep your budget, vacation style, and desired facilities in mind. Luxury lodges give unequaled levels of luxury and service, and mid-range alternatives strike a reasonable mix between comfort and budget. Budget-friendly campgrounds and homestays are ideal for adventurous tourists looking for a more rustic experience.

Pro Tip: Whatever accommodation you choose, book well in advance, particularly during the high season (June to August and December to February). Queen Elizabeth National Park is a popular location, so accommodations fill up fast.

So there you have it. With this thorough reference to animal watching, boat tours, and lodging alternatives, you'll be well on your way to creating an outstanding safari experience in Queen Elizabeth National Park. Remember, it's more than simply checking off creatures on your list; it's about connecting with nature, appreciating wildlife, and making experiences that will last a lifetime.

Chapter 11: Beyond the Parks: Revealing Uganda's Soul (and Perhaps Mastering the Art of Matoke)

Alright, adrenaline seekers! We've completed amazing safaris, hiked through jungles in pursuit of gorillas, and navigated the busy streets of Kampala. But Uganda's charm stretches well beyond its national parks. This chapter goes into the core of Ugandan culture, providing unique experiences that will leave you with a better knowledge and respect for this amazing nation.

11.1 Homestay Experiences in Rural Uganda: A Hilarious Immersion (and Perhaps a Few Mosquito Bites).

For a true Ugandan experience, avoid the tourist path and enjoy the warmth of a homestay! Imagine yourself ensconced in a traditional hamlet, surrounded by rolling hills and lush vegetation. You'll be greeted by a Ugandan family, share meals cooked over an open fire, learn a few basic Luganda words (believe me, trying the language will keep your hosts entertained for hours!), and get a personal look at Ugandan life. Now, full disclosure (since honesty is essential!), a homestay may not be for everyone. Here's a preview glimpse at what you may expect, with a good dose of humor:

The Rustic Charm (and Possible Challenges):
Accommodation: Think simple yet comfy. You may be sleeping on a woven mat or a modest bed with a mosquito net (those little guys may be tenacious, so bring some repellent!).

Bathroom Facilities: Let's just say that it may not be a five-star spa experience. Accept the bucket showers and community facilities; it's all part of the trip!

The Power Situation: In rural regions, electricity supply might be intermittent. Enjoy the chance to disconnect, stargaze under the Milky Way, and share tales by the flickering firelight.

During my homestay journey, I sought to impress my host family with my newly acquired Luganda abilities. I proudly announced at breakfast, "Mwatudde!" which I thought meant "good morning." Turns out, in my enthusiasm, I'd accidentally declared, "I'm full!" The entire family burst out laughing, and let's just say, my Ugandan vocabulary lessons continued well into the evening (with a healthy dose of amusement from them).

The Rewards (and They Are Priceless):

Despite the odd power outage or language misunderstanding, a homestay provides an unrivaled chance to engage with Ugandan culture. You will feel the warmth of Ugandan hospitality, learn about their customs, and see their way of life. Imagine assisting in the preparation of a traditional supper (be prepared to learn the skill of matoke, mashed green bananas, a Ugandan staple!), taking part in a vibrant drumming session, or just exchanging tales with your newfound family beneath the starry sky. These are the moments that leave a lasting impression and a greater respect for Uganda's essence.

Homestay experiences may be arranged via local tour companies or non-governmental organizations (NGOs) that operate in rural areas. Choose a trustworthy organization that focuses on ethical tourism and fair remuneration for homestay families.

11.2 Traditional Ugandan Crafts and Souvenirs: Beyond the T-Shirt

Are you looking for a one-of-a-kind keepsake to commemorate your Uganda adventure? Skip the bland t-shirts and explore the world of authentic Ugandan crafts! Here are some hidden treasures to include on your shopping list:

Bark Cloth: This traditional cloth, fashioned from the bark of certain trees, has complex patterns and brilliant colors. It's a lovely and ecological keepsake that benefits local craftspeople.

Basketry: Ugandan baskets are more than simply useful; they are pieces of beauty! Woven from natural materials like sisal and raffia, they are available in a variety of sizes and shapes, making them ideal for keeping valuables or adding a bit of Ugandan flare to your house.

Ugandan beading ranges from elaborate necklaces and bracelets to bright wall hangings, demonstrating a lively show of artistry. Support your local craftsmen and locate a one-of-a-kind artwork that appeals to you.

Wood Carvings: Using indigenous wood, skilled Ugandan artists create magnificent sculptures and figures. Look for carvings of animals, traditional masks, or commonplace things, all with a tale to tell.

Pro tip: Expect to haggle in Ugandan marketplaces. Do it with a smile and courtesy, and you may be able to get a great price on a one-of-a-kind keepsake.

11.3 Experiencing Ugandan Cuisine & Cooking Classes: A Culinary Adventure (with Maybe a Little Spice)

Ugandan cuisine is a delectable combination of tastes, textures, and fragrances. Move over, dull airport food! Here is what awaiting your taste buds:

Matoke (Mashed Green Bananas): This Ugandan dish is a must-try. Matoke may be boiled, steamed, fried, or roasted, and is used in a variety of cuisines. Prepare for a fresh spin on the simple banana!

Rolex: Don't be deceived by the name; this Ugandan street dish is anything from elegant. Consider a chapati filled with delicious ingredients such as veggies, meats, or even fried eggs. It's a tasty and inexpensive way to sample Ugandan cuisine on the fly.

Luwombo (cooked Stew): This tasty cuisine consists of meats, vegetables, and spices cooked in banana leaves. The banana leaves provide a gentle sweetness and perfume, giving Luwombo a genuinely unique gastronomic experience.

Grasshoppers (Optional Adventure): Are you feeling adventurous? Try some fried grasshoppers, a famous Ugandan food. Don't criticize it till you try it; they're pleasantly crispy and protein-rich!

Taking Cooking Class:
The best approach to learning about Ugandan food is to take a cooking lesson. Imagine yourself in a local kitchen, learning the secrets to these delectable delicacies from a Ugandan mom or papa. You will learn not just culinary skills, but also about Ugandan culture and customs. Plus, you get to consume your creations at the end - a win-win!

During my Ugandan culinary lesson, I misjudged the strength of chili. I overzealously added some to my Luwombo, causing the whole dish to ignite! Let's just say that my students had a nice chuckle at my expense (and with lots of water, we were able to put out the flames). Regardless of the original incident, the outcome was a fantastic and memorable supper.

Part 3:

Exploring Rwanda

Chapter 12: Kigali: A Modern City Rich in History

Kigali isn't the usual African capital. Sure, it boasts busy marketplaces brimming with colorful textiles and streets throbbing with motorcycles (affectionately termed "taxis motos" - ready for a crazy, but exciting ride if you dare!). However, underlying this sophisticated exterior is a rich tapestry of history, most notably the terrible chapter of the 1994 Rwandan Genocide.

However, Kigali is a city that refuses to be defined by its history. It's a place where resilience and optimism reign supreme. Skyscrapers pierce the skyline, chic cafés pour out into cobblestone streets, and art galleries reflect a nation's revived inventiveness.

12.1 Kigali Genocide Memorial & Learning about Rwanda's Past: A Journey of Remembrance (and Perhaps Some Tears)

Now, here's the thing: comprehending Rwanda's history is essential for completely appreciating its tremendous progress. The Kigali Genocide Memorial is a dramatic and moving remembrance of the horrible events of 1994. It's not an easy visit, but it's important.

Imagine strolling through tranquil gardens, the air saturated with the aroma of reminiscence. Exhibits commemorating the lives lost and the tales of surviving emerge in front of you. Prepare to drop a tear or two (don't worry, even the most seasoned traveler may get a lump in their throat). But, among the misery, there is a glimmer of optimism. The monument emphasizes the power of forgiveness and healing, reflecting Rwanda's steadfast spirit.

Now, I'll confess that when I went to the memorial, I wasn't expecting such an emotional rollercoaster. I was walking through the exhibits, all sad and introspective, when I heard a loud sniffle behind me. I turned around to see a fellow visitor, a huge biker male with a full-sleeve tattoo, wiping his tears with a crumpled tissue. We locked eyes for a minute, and a wordless understanding passed between us. Here we were, two perfect strangers pulled together by a poignant encounter. It was a striking reminder of the universality of human emotions and the significance of remembering the past to create a greater tomorrow. **But Kigali offers so much more!**

Don't let history eclipse Kigali's liveliness now. After you visit the monument, travel to a rooftop pub with panoramic city views and have a Rwandan beer. In the evenings, attend a live music performance at a local hotspot and experience Kigali's vibrant nightlife. There are museums dedicated to Rwandan art and culture, lively marketplaces where you can negotiate for gifts (with a smile, of course!), and fashionable cafés selling great Rwandan coffee.

By the time you leave Kigali, you'll have a renewed respect for this amazing city. It's a place where history is recognized, the present is honored, and the future is full of promise. So prepare to explore, learn, and be inspired by Kigali's enchantment!

12.2 Museums and Cultural Sites in Kigali: Exploring Rwandan History and Creativity

Kigali has a remarkable variety of cultural events outside the Genocide Memorial. The following museums and historical places will reveal Rwanda's rich tapestry:

Inema Art Institution: This colorful institution exhibits modern Rwandan art, including sculptures, paintings, photography, and installations. Prepare to be inspired by Rwanda's budding artists' ability and inventiveness. (Address: KN 3 Ave, Kigali, Rwanda. Open Tuesday through Sunday, 10 a.m. to 5 p.m.)

The Ivuka Foundation is dedicated to preserving the legacy of the Rwandan Genocide and provides guided tours and courses. Discover the history of the genocide, the experiences of survivors, and Rwanda's path to reconciliation. (Address: KG 1 Ave, Kigali, Rwanda. Open Tuesday through Saturday, 8:30 a.m. to 5 p.m.)

The Presidential Palace Museum, housed in President Habyarimana's old mansion, offers a glimpse into Rwandan history. The exhibits depict the progress of Rwanda's government and the country's route to prosperity. (Address: KG 2 Ave, Kigali, Rwanda. Open Tuesday through Sunday, 9 a.m. to 5 p.m.)

Belgian Colonial Residence: Step back in time to the Belgian Colonial Residence, which is now the National Institute of Museums of Rwanda. This colonial-era structure includes relics and exhibits from Rwanda's pre-colonial history and the Belgian colonial period. (Address: KG 6 Ave, Kigali, Rwanda. Open Tuesday through Sunday, 9 a.m. to 5 p.m.)

Pro Tip: Many museums in Kigali offer combination tickets, which enable you to visit many institutions at a subsidized rate.

12.3 Exploring Kigali's Art Scene and Restaurants: A Feast for the Senses

Kigali is a growing city, and its thriving art scene reflects that. Here are some must-sees for art enthusiasts and foodies alike:

Inema Art café: This contemporary café, situated inside the Inema Art Center, is a refuge for creatives. Enjoy great Rwandan coffee and pastries while appreciating modern art exhibitions. (Address: KN 3 Ave, Kigali, Rwanda. Open Tuesday through Sunday, 8 a.m. to 10 p.m.)

Milles Collines Hotel: Enjoy a drink at the Kigali Serena Hotel, which was once known as the Milles Collines Hotel. This old hotel played a critical part in the genocide by sheltering over 1,200 individuals. Enjoy a beverage and magnificent city views while learning about the hotel's fascinating history. (Address: KG7 Ave, Kigali, Rwanda)

Zenith Cafe: This busy restaurant serves superb Rwandan and international food in a bright setting. Ideal for a relaxed lunch or supper, with an outside dining area where you can people-watch. (Address: KG 15 Ave, Kigali, Rwanda. Open every day from 8 a.m. to 11 p.m.)

Repub Lounge: Enjoy a touch of luxury at the Repub Lounge, which is recognized for its trendy environment and delicious drinks. An excellent choice for a pre-dinner drink or a night out with friends. (Address: KG 22 Ave, Kigali, Rwanda. Open Tuesday through Sunday, 5 p.m. to 2 a.m.)

Bonus Tip: Don't pass on eating Rwandan street cuisine! Try brochettes (grilled meat skewers), "sambosas" (savory pastries with a Rwandan twist), and fresh tropical fruits to get a sense of the local cuisine.

These are only the beginnings of discovering Kigali's cultural and gastronomic scene. Kigali's ever-changing art scene and intriguing eateries cater to every taste bud and excite the creative spirit. So, stroll the streets, uncover hidden jewels, and savor the many tastes of this magnificent city!

Chapter 13: Volcanoes National Park: Mountain Gorilla Trekking in the Mist!

Prepare yourself for an incredible journey! In this chapter, we explore the center of Volcanoes National Park in Rwanda in quest of the spectacular mountain gorillas. Imagine yourself hiking through lush jungles, the air heavy with excitement, until you come face to face with these gentle giants. It's an experience that will live with you forever.

13.1 Gorilla Trekking Permits and Booking Information: Securing Your Once-in-a-Lifetime Experience

First things first: gorilla permits are required for hiking. Volcanoes National Park rigorously regulates the number of visitors per gorilla group daily to maintain responsible tourism and gorilla health. Here's how you can reserve your spot:

Booking: The Rwanda Development Board (RDB) manages permits. Bookings may be made online via their official website or with reputable tour companies. Booking is essential, particularly during the high season (June to August and December to February). Permits sometimes sell out months in advance, so do not wait!

Cost: Gorilla trekking permits are not inexpensive, but the experience is invaluable. Permits presently cost US $1500 per person, per day. Consider this a contribution to conservation efforts and the survival of these endangered monkeys.

Pro Tip: For a multifaceted Rwandan vacation, combine your gorilla trekking permit with other activities in Rwanda, such as chimp tracking in Nyungwe National Park.

13.2 What to Expect on a Gorilla Trek in Volcanoes National Park: An Experience Like No Other

Okay, the permit has been acquired, your hiking boots have been laced, and excitement is building in your gut. Here's what you can expect on your gorilla trek:

Prepare for an early morning wake-up call. Treks normally begin at 7:00 a.m., enabling you to find the gorillas before they disperse for the day.

Meeting Your Guides: You will be given a team of professional and qualified park rangers to accompany you through the jungle and assure your safety during the walk.

Into the Lush Rainforest: The walk itself is an experience. Imagine winding trails through dense bamboo forests, the air filled with the sounds of birds and insects. The terrain can be uneven and muddy, so good physical fitness is required.

The Encounter: And then the magical moment occurs. Following the gorillas' footprints will bring you face-to-face with a family group. Observe how they interact, groom each other, and play with their young. This is a very humbling and memorable experience.

Important Reminder: You are a visitor in the gorillas' environment. Maintain a respectful distance of at least 7 meters and avoid making loud sounds or unexpected movements. Before the hike, your guide will go over the correct etiquette with you.

13.3 Responsible Gorilla Trekking Practices: Be a Force of Good

Gorilla trekking is a privilege, yet with it comes responsibility. Here are some ways you may have a good influence on both yourself and the gorillas:

Choose Responsible Tour Operators: Book your trip with a reputed firm that is dedicated to gorilla conservation and sustainable methods. Look for companies that promote local communities and use certified guides.

Respect the Habitat: Stay on authorized routes to prevent damaging the sensitive rainforest ecology. Leave no trace by packing away all of your waste and avoiding using any dangerous chemicals around the gorillas, such as DEET-containing bug repellents.

Minimize Your Impact: Limit the use of cameras with flashes, since this might upset the gorillas. Capture your moments using conventional camera settings and zoom lenses.

By following these habits, you may help safeguard the survival of these amazing species for centuries to come. Remember that going gorilla trekking is more than simply crossing something off your bucket list; it's about contributing to conservation efforts and witnessing nature's pristine beauty.

Chapter 14: Nyungwe Forest National Park: Discovering a Realm of Emerald Magic

While the mountain gorillas steal the show in Volcanoes National Park, Rwanda provides another fantastic wildlife experience waiting to be explored: chimpanzee trekking in Nyungwe Forest National Park. This chapter takes you into the heart of this green paradise, where towering trees shelter playful chimpanzees, stunning canopy treks await, and a broad range of animals flourishes.

14.1 Chimpanzee Tracking Permits and Booking Information: Meeting Our Closest Cousins

Imagine trekking into Nyungwe's deep woods, listening for chimpanzee sounds echoing across the treetops. Observing these sophisticated monkeys in their natural surroundings is an unforgettable experience. Here's how to get it done:

Permits and Booking: Chimpanzee tracking permits, like gorilla trekking, are necessary. You may get them via the Rwanda Development Board (RDB) website or from reputable travel companies. Booking in advance is required, particularly during high seasons.

Cost: Chimpanzee trekking permits are less expensive than gorilla permits, costing around $90 per person for each hike.

Pro Tip: For the ultimate Rwandan primate experience, combine your chimp trekking with a visit to Volcanoes National Park!

14.2 Exploring the Nyungwe Forest Canopy Walk: A Bird's Eye View of the Rainforest

Nyungwe National Park provides more than simply interactions with our closest ape cousins. Strap on your adventure spirit and ready to fly into the rainforest canopy on a thrilling suspended walkway!

A Breathtaking Experience: Imagine walking along a network of elevated pathways that soar high above the forest floor. The Nyungwe Forest Canopy Walk provides panoramic views of the green expanse, letting you glimpse birds, monkeys, and other species from an unusual vantage point.

Suitable for All Ages: This exercise is appropriate for all ages and fitness levels. The pathways are solid and well-kept, guaranteeing a safe and pleasurable experience for everybody.

Bonus Tip: As you stroll through the canopy, look for colorful birds like the Ruwenzori Turaco and the gorgeous Blue Monkey.

14.3 Biodiversity and Wildlife Viewing in Nyungwe National Park: A Land of Riches

Nyungwe National Park is a biodiversity hotspot, with over 1300 species of plants and animals. Here's an example of the amazing species you could encounter:

The chimpanzees are, of course, the show's main attraction. Observe as they swing through the trees, groom each other, and demonstrate their lively personalities.

Other Primates: Keep a watch out for colobus monkeys with their striking black and white coats, as well as shy golden monkeys with their characteristic golden pelage.

Birdwatching Paradise: Nyungwe is a birdwatcher's paradise, with over 1300 species. Look for brightly colored turacos, secretive francolins, and even the unusual shoebill stork.

Small Mammals: The forest floor is brimming with life. You could see shy antelope species, inquisitive rodents, and a variety of beautiful butterflies.

A Final Note:
Nyungwe National Park provides a one-of-a-kind chance to explore an emerald green environment, interact with interesting species, and enjoy Rwanda's extraordinary biodiversity. Whether you're following chimps, flying over the canopy, or just admiring the grandeur of the rainforest, Nyungwe guarantees an amazing trip.

Chapter 15: Akagera National Park: Wildlife Safaris in Rwanda's Savannah

Hold on to your hats, nature aficionados! We're leaving the verdant embrace of Nyungwe Forest for the vast savannas of Akagera National Park. Lions roar, zebras graze, and a wide variety of species await discovery. Prepare for an exciting safari journey into the heart of Rwanda.

15.1 Wildlife Viewing Opportunities in Akagera National Park: A feast for the eyes.

Akagera National Park has a spectacular turnaround story. Once extremely depleted, the park has undertaken a successful recovery effort, attracting a diverse range of animals. Here are some of the spectacular wildlife you may meet on your safari:

The Big Five (Almost): Akagera is home to four of the Big Five, including lions, elephants, buffaloes, and rhinos (reintroduced in 2017). While seeing a leopard may be a rare occurrence, the park provides a fantastic opportunity to view these gorgeous creatures.

Grazers Abound: Zebras with distinguishing stripes, graceful giraffes straining for leaves from the topmost trees, and herds of antelopes such as the exquisite topi and timid bushbuck occupy the savannas.

Predators on the Prowl: Keep an eye out for lions lounging in the heat, cheetahs running across the plains, and spotted hyenas looking for their next meal.
Avian Abundance: The skies over Akagera are alive with birds. Look for bright storks, beautiful eagles flying on thermals, and a variety of brilliant songbirds.

Pro Tip: Early mornings and late afternoons are ideal for wildlife watching since animals are more active during these colder hours.

15.2 Game Drives and Safaris in Akagera National Park: Discovering the Wild

Safaris are the finest way to explore the marvels of Akagera National Park. Here are some choices to consider:

Morning and afternoon game drives: These traditional safaris take place in open-air vehicles, letting you get up close (but safely!) to the park's animals. Experienced guides will lead you around the park, offering their expertise and pointing out creatures.

Boat Cruises on Lake Ihema: Take a picturesque boat excursion over Lake Ihema, Rwanda's biggest lake. This is an excellent chance to see hippos lazing in the sun, crocodiles hiding in the shallows, and a variety of water birds.

Night Game Drives: on an exciting experience, go on a night game drive. Observe nocturnal wildlife like lions with blazing eyes, secretive leopards on the prowl, and a symphony of evening species serenading the savanna.

Important tips: Always adhere to your guide's recommendations and keep a safe distance from wild animals.

15.3 Park Entrance Fees and Booking Information

All park visitors must pay an admission charge. These fees support park upkeep and conservation activities. You may get your access permit at the park's entrance gate or from trustworthy tour companies who will manage the logistics for you.

Tip: Combine your Akagera National Park safari with a visit to Volcanoes National Park or Nyungwe Forest National Park for a well-rounded Rwandan vacation that includes both monkeys and savanna encounters.

15.4 Accommodation Options Near Akagera National Park.

Akagera National Park has a wide range of housing alternatives to suit all budgets and interests. This is a brief guide:

Luxury Lodges: If you want an exceptional experience, try staying at one of Akagera's deluxe lodges. These resorts provide breathtaking vistas, exceptional service, and high-quality facilities.

Mid-Range Lodges: Several mid-range lodges provide comfortable lodgings and wonderful meals in a picturesque location, making them ideal for budget-conscious guests.

Camping: The park offers camping possibilities for those who are adventurous. Imagine falling asleep beneath a starry sky and waking up to the sounds of the African jungle.

Pro Tip: Accommodations tend to fill up fast, particularly during peak season. Book your stay in advance, particularly if you have your heart set on a particular lodge.

Chapter 16: Genocide Memorials and Cultural Sites: Reflecting on Rwanda's Past

Rwanda's story is a tapestry made with strands of perseverance, optimism, and a strong determination to never forget the past. This chapter looks into the Kigali Genocide Memorial, a painful reminder of the tragic days of 1994, as well as various cultural events that provide insight into Rwanda's lively spirit today.

16.1 Kigali Genocide Memorial: A Place of Remembrance (A Journey Through History and Emotion)

The Kigali Genocide Memorial is more than simply a structure; it is a strong tribute to the human spirit's capacity to survive and rebuild. Prepare to go on a trip through history that may leave you in tears, but ultimately optimistic.

Walking Through Serene Gardens: Imagine visiting the memorial grounds. Tranquil gardens with well-kept grass and bright flowers provide a feeling of calm in sharp contrast to the atrocities it recalls. Take a deep breath; the displays ahead will elicit a variety of emotions.

Unveiling the Stories: The permanent exhibition is presented in a succession of well-curated presentations. Heartbreaking photographs, human stories, and historical artifacts provide a vivid picture of the events before and during the genocide. Prepare to learn about the origins of ethnic conflict, media manipulation, and the plunge into bloodshed. There are other exhibits depicting heroic deeds, as well as tales of regular individuals who risked their lives to help others.

A Sea of Faces: One of the most moving areas is the Children's Room. Rows and rows of miniature photographs look back at you, a somber reminder of the innocent souls lost. It's an agonizing moment, a clear reminder of the human cost of hate.

A Flame of Hope: The memorial grounds include the ultimate resting place for more than 250,000 people. Descend into the crypt, a silent spot full of solemn regard. Here, you may offer your respects and reflect on the tragedy's gravity. Despite the sadness, there is a glimmer of optimism. The monument is a daily reminder of the value of forgiveness, reconciliation, and creating a brighter future.

During my visit to the memorial, I found myself strolling around the displays, utterly fascinated by the tales. Tears welled up in my eyes as I read a little girl's journal post, which detailed her anxiety and uncertainty. Suddenly, a delicate hand stroked my shoulder. I glanced up to see a fellow guest, an older lady with gentle eyes, give a subtle nod of agreement. At that time, words were unneeded. We shared empathy and pain. It served as a reminder that, even amid great sorrow, mankind can find consolation and community.

More than Just a Memorial: The Kigali Genocide Memorial is an important milestone in Rwanda's rehabilitation process. It acts as a hub for teaching, raising awareness, and avoiding future tragedies. It is also a place for survivors to grieve and families to find closure.

16.2 Additional Genocide Memorial Sites in Rwanda

The Kigali Genocide Memorial is a national focal point, but other tragic places around Rwanda pay honor to the victims. Here are a few worth visiting:

Nyamata Church: This former church, now a mass grave, serves as a terrible reminder of the genocide's cruelty. More than 5,000 individuals were slaughtered here, and their skeletal remains are still preserved behind the church walls.

Murambi Technical Institution: Another terrible location, this institution served as a killing ground during the genocide. Exhibits depict the tools used and the victims' experiences.

Bisesero Memorial: This site remembers Bisesero's valiant resistance warriors, who battled against tremendous odds for more than two months.

Important tips: Visiting these areas might be emotionally stressful. Take your time, be courteous, and allow yourself to process any feelings that may surface.

16.3 Cultural Experiences in Rwanda: Beyond the Shadow of History.

Rwanda is not defined just by its history. It's a country full of lively culture and customs. Here are a few methods to immerse oneself in the heart of Rwandan culture:

Traditional Dance Performances: Experience the electric intensity of Rwandan dance troupes. Be mesmerized by the rhythmic drumming, complex footwork, and vibrant costumes. You could even be encouraged to participate (don't worry, no previous expertise is necessary; just embrace the spirit!).

My Attempt at Intore Dance (A Hilarious Fumble): During my stay, I couldn't pass up the chance to attend a traditional dance workshop. We were exposed to the "Intore" dance, a dramatic exhibition done by males in the style of warriors. Now, I'm a reasonably coordinated person, but those Rwandan dancers made it seem simple! As I endeavored to grasp the complicated footwork and coordinated stomps, I resembled a young giraffe attempting to walk rather than a powerful warrior. The other participants, bless their souls, tried not to laugh too much. Despite my comedic bumbling, it was a joyful and meaningful experience, allowing me to interact with the local culture while also admiring the passion and ability of these exceptional dancers.

Village Visits: Get out of the city and experience a typical Rwandan village. Meet the people, learn about their way of life, and see age-old traditions such as basket weaving and pottery production. You may even be encouraged to try your hand at these crafts (be prepared for some friendly laughs at your first tries!).

A Thousand Hills for a Thousand Words: Immerse yourself in Rwanda's spectacular environment by hiking through the picturesque "A Thousand Hills." This network of undulating hills provides panoramic views, opportunities to observe native birds and animals, and insight into rural Rwandan life.

Coffee Tours and Tastings: Rwanda is known for its high-quality coffee. Take a coffee farm tour, learn about the bean-to-cup process, and enjoy the rich scent and exquisite flavor of a Rwandan cup of coffee. It's the ideal way to relax after a day of traveling and makes an excellent keepsake to take home.

Embracing these cultural experiences can help you obtain a better grasp of Rwanda's colorful tapestry. You'll see its people's resiliency, steadfast passion, and resolve to create a better future.

Chapter 17: Accommodation Options (Budget to Luxury): Find Your Rwandan Refuge

Rwanda has a wide range of hotel alternatives to suit any budget or travel style, from backpacker hostels to lavish safari lodges. Here's a detailed guide to help you choose the ideal Rwandan hideaway.

17.1 Budget Accommodation Options in Uganda and Rwanda: Keeping it Simple but Comfortable

Budget tourists should rejoice! Rwanda caters to the budget-conscious explorer with a variety of inexpensive alternatives that will not break the bank.

Guest Houses and Hostels: These communal and welcoming lodgings provide bunk beds or basic private rooms at extremely inexpensive rates. Expect public facilities and common spaces, which are ideal for meeting other tourists and exchanging tales. Prices normally vary between $10 and $25 each night.

Examples in Uganda include Red Chili Backpackers (Kampala), The Hive Coliving Hostel (Kampala), and Backpackers Paradise (Lake Bunyonyi).

Examples in Rwanda include Yego House Kigali, The Hut Hostel (Kigali), and Distant Horizon Guest House (Kibuye).

Campsites and cheap Lodges: Enjoy the outdoors and reconnect with nature at a campground or a cheap lodge. These choices provide modest facilities such as shared restrooms and common kitchens, but they also include gorgeous sites and the opportunity to explore Rwandan nature. Camping or modest rooms often cost between $20 and $40 per night.

Examples in Uganda include Murchison River Lodge Campsite (Murchison Falls National Park), Ichumbi Gorilla Lodge Campsite (Bwindi Impenetrable National Park), and Lake Bunyonyi Eco-Camp.

Examples in Rwanda include Muhabura Hostel (Musanze), Kinigi Guest House (Volcanoes National Park), and Nyungwe Hillside Camp (Nyungwe National Park).

Tips for Budget Travel:

Consider location: Kigali's accommodations are often more costly than those in smaller towns. If you are on a limited budget, consider lodging outside of the city center.

Use public transportation: Rwanda has a decent network of buses and minibusses. Taking public transportation might save you money over taxis or private vehicles.

Self-catering: Choosing guesthouses with kitchens enables you to cook your meals, which is a big cost-saving option. Purchase food from local markets for fresh and inexpensive items.

17.2 Mid-Range Accommodation Options in Uganda and Rwanda: Achieving the Ideal Balance

Mid-range hotels and lodges provide an excellent blend of comfort and facilities.

Mid-Range Hotels: These hotels provide comfortable rooms with en-suite bathrooms, air conditioning (in certain instances), and standard facilities such as on-site restaurants and laundry services. Prices normally vary between $50 and $100 each night.

Examples in Uganda include Speke Apartments Kampala (Kampala), Cassia Cottage (Queen Elizabeth National Park), and Mburo Green Paradise (Lake Mburo National Park).

Examples in Rwanda: Kigali Marriott Hotel (Kigali), Mountain Gorilla View Lodge (Musanze), and Paradise Guesthouse (Kibuye).

Staying in a mid-range lodge allows you to immerse yourself in nature. These places provide cozy cottages or bungalows, beautiful natural locations, and often incorporate activities such as nature walks or guided excursions. Prices normally vary between $100 and $200 each night.

Examples in Uganda include Mahogany Springs Lodge (Bwindi Impenetrable National Park), Ishasha Wilderness Camp (Queen Elizabeth National Park), and Chobe Safari Lodge (Murchison Falls National Park).
Examples in Rwanda include the One & Only Nyungwe House (Nyungwe National Park), Magashi

Camp (Akagera National Park), and Sabyinyo Silverback Lodge (Volcanoes National Park).

Tips for Middle-Range Travelers:
Read reviews: Before reserving your stay, check internet reviews to get a sense of the environment, facilities, and value for money.

Consider all-inclusive packages: Some mid-range resorts include all-inclusive meals, activities, and park admission. This may be a handy and cost-effective solution.

Compare prices: Prices vary based on the season and location. Shop around and compare prices before making a final selection.

17.3 Luxury Lodges & Camps in Uganda & Rwanda: Unforgettable Experiences in Unique Style

For those looking for the ultimate Rwandan (and Ugandan) experience, luxury hotels and camps provide unrivaled comfort, service, and exclusivity. Imagine yourself ensconced in a secluded cabin overlooking a gorilla habitat, dining on gourmet meals cooked by world-class chefs, and going on bespoke safaris with skilled guides. Prepare to be spoiled!

Luxury Lodges: These magnificent retreats are redefining the notion of housing. Consider private infinity pools with stunning views, huge suites outfitted with every conceivable comfort, and superb customized service. Expect top-tier restaurants serving worldwide cuisine with a Rwandan flair, as well as on-site spas providing revitalizing treatments. Prices generally range from $500 per night to several thousand dollars for the most luxurious houses.

Examples in Uganda: Clouds Mountain Gorilla Lodge (Bwindi Impenetrable National Park), Chephene Camp (Queen Elizabeth National Park), and Apoka Lodge (Kidepo Valley National Park).

Examples (Rwanda) include Bisate Lodge (Volcanoes National Park), Singita Kwitonda Lodge (Volcanoes National Park), and One&Only Gorilla's Nest.

Luxury Tented Camps: For an unforgettable and immersive experience, try staying in a luxury-tented camp. These luxurious lodgings provide all of the amenities of a luxury resort while maintaining the romantic atmosphere of a safari camp. Imagine sleeping beneath a starry sky, listening to the sounds of the African wild, yet enjoying sumptuous furniture, private bathrooms, and superb service. Prices often vary between $800 and $1,500 per night.

Examples in Uganda include the Kyambura Gorge Luxury Tented Camp in Queen Elizabeth National Park, the Mahali Mgahinga Safari Camp in Bwindi Impenetrable National Park, and the Nile Safari Lodge in Murchison Falls National Park.

Examples in Rwanda include Magena Gorilla Lodge (Volcanoes National Park) and Bush Camp Masai Mara (Akagera National Park).

Tips For Luxury Travelers:

Book in advance: Luxury lodges and campers fill up fast, particularly during peak season. Plan your journey ahead of time and book your accommodations early.

Consider inclusions: Some luxury resorts include all-inclusive packages that include meals, beverages, activities, park fees, and even laundry services. This may be a handy and cost-effective solution.

Choose your experience: Luxury lodges and campers cater to a variety of interests. Some specialize in gorilla trekking, while others provide excellent wildlife-watching chances in the savannas. Select a home that is compatible with your interests.

Note on Responsible Luxury:

Many luxury resorts and camps in Rwanda and Uganda are devoted to environmentally friendly methods and responsible tourism. They collaborate with local people, reduce their environmental effects, and promote conservation. Consider this while making your decision, and choose qualities that reflect your ideals.

Chapter 18: Dining: A Culinary Adventure Through Uganda and Rwanda.

Prepare to savor the gastronomic delicacies of Uganda and Rwanda! From rich stews to fresh tropical fruits, these nations' food is colorful and savory, leaving you wanting more.

18.1 Must-Try Ugandan Dishes: A Fusion Of Flavors

Ugandan cuisine is a magnificent combination of influences that reflects the country's rich history and ethnic diversity. Here are some must-try foods to include on your Ugandan cuisine itinerary:

Matooke (Green Banana Stew) is a Ugandan staple. Green bananas are steamed or cooked until soft, then mashed into a filling and somewhat sour stew. It is often served with stewed vegetables, beans, or a tasty peanut sauce. Matooke is known as "green gold" due to its widespread popularity.

Rolex (Rolled Eggs): Despite its name, this Ugandan street snack is far from sophisticated. Imagine a fluffy omelet topped with a fried egg, chopped veggies (such as onions, tomatoes, and peppers), and sometimes sausage or cheese. It's a tasty and inexpensive on-the-go breakfast or snack. ***My Rolex Revelation:** On a busy Kampala street corner, I saw a hawker masterfully flip a Rolex with a flourish. Intrigued, I tried a mouthful and was immediately hooked! The textures and tastes worked so well together that it was impossible to refuse.*

Luwombo (Steamed Stew): This meal is a culinary delight. Marinated meat, fish, or vegetables are cooked on banana leaves, which retain moisture and provide a mild banana taste. When you open the scented gift, you're delighted by a delicate and savory stew, which pairs well with Ugandan posho (cornmeal porridge).

Fried grasshoppers (nsenene) are a must-try for every adventurous diner in Uganda. These crunchy insects are surprisingly good when seasoned with spices and chile, and they are a common bar snack or street dish. Confession: I was first apprehensive about trying nsenene. But, prompted by my Ugandan travel buddies, I took a leap of faith. And, guess what? They were extremely good! The crunchy texture and salty taste were unexpectedly irresistible.

18.2 Must-Try Rwandan Dishes: Celebrating Freshness

Rwandan cuisine is noted for its simplicity and focus on fresh, locally sourced ingredients. Here are some foods you shouldn't miss:

Ibiryanko (Spicy Grilled Meat Skewers): Marinated cubes of beef, poultry, or goat are skewered and cooked to perfection. These delicious skewers are usually served with kachumbari, a Rwandan salsa prepared from tomatoes, onions, chili peppers, and fresh herbs. Be ready for a taste explosion!

Isombe (Leaf Stew): This bright green stew is a Rwandan staple. It is made using a variety of leafy green vegetables, such as cassava leaves or spinach, and is often spiced with chiles, peanuts, and, on occasion, fish or pork. Isombe is a healthful and tasty meal that is usually eaten with rice or plantains.

Brochettes (Grilled Skewers): Like the ibiryanko, brochettes are a popular Rwandan street snack. Marinated meat, fish, or vegetables are skewered and grilled over high heat. The smokey taste and range of flavors make them ideal for a fast and delicious snack.

Akabanga (Sweet Potatoes with Peanut Sauce): This simple yet wonderful meal exemplifies the charm of Rwandan cuisine. Boiled sweet potatoes are coated in a rich and fragrant peanut sauce, resulting in a delectable blend of sweet and savory tastes. Pro tip: Don't pass up the opportunity to eat Rwandan peanuts! They are renowned for their distinct taste and are often offered roasted by street sellers.

18.3 Vegetarian and Vegan Dining Options: A World of Flavor Awaits.

While Ugandan and Rwandan cuisines are primarily meat-based, there are plenty of vegetarian and vegan alternatives to suit every taste. Here's what you may expect:

Abundant veggies: Both Uganda and Rwanda have a large range of fresh veggies. Expect meals with eggplant, green beans, sweet potatoes, mushrooms, and okra, which are often prepared in stews, stir-fries, or served grilled.

Pulses galore: Beans and lentils are common protein sources in vegetarian Rwandan and Ugandan cuisine. Use them in stews, soups, or as a stuffing for savory pancakes.

Plantains (Matoke or Matooke): This multipurpose starchy fruit is a vegetarian favorite. Plantains may be boiled, mashed, fried, or roasted, providing a variety of tasty alternatives. Try matoke (green plantains) mashed into a full meal, or enjoy sweet, fried ripe plantains for a treat.

Beyond the Plate: Rwandan Dining Adventure

Dining in Rwanda is a social experience as well as a culinary one. Expect to be greeted cordially and to enjoy meals with family, friends, or maybe new travel companions. Here are a few things to remember:

Etiquette Tip: Wash your hands before eating. Food is traditionally eaten with your right hand, and it is courteous to wait until everyone at the table has been served before diving in.

Sharing is Caring: Rwandan meals are often communal, with dishes placed in the middle of the table for everybody to enjoy. Prepare to taste a little of everything!

Second helpings? Absolutely! Don't be bashful about asking for more. Refusing a second helping might be seen as an indication that you didn't like your dinner.
So, come hungry and with an open mind to your gastronomic trip to Uganda and Rwanda. From street cuisine delights to sentimental stews, these nations provide a delectable sample of Africa that will excite your taste buds and leave you with unforgettable memories!

Chapter 19: Staying Connected (Internet Access and Phone Usage)

Staying connected in today's globe is critical, especially while on an adventure in Rwanda. This chapter will walk you through your internet and phone choices, ensuring that you can share your adventures, keep in contact with loved ones, and obtain critical information throughout your journey.

19.1 Internet Access and SIM Card Options: Connecting with the World

Rwanda has made considerable advances in improving its telecommunications infrastructure. Here's how to keep connected with the web:

Mobile Internet: This is the most convenient method to use the internet in Rwanda. Upon arriving, obtain a local SIM card from one of the main mobile network providers, such as MTN Rwanda or Airtel Rwanda. Both provide prepaid SIM cards with a variety of data bundles to meet your requirements.

Here is a short comparison.

Provider coverage and typical data package prices.

MTN Rwanda has extensive network coverage across the nation, with plans starting at $5 for a few GB.

Airtel Rwanda has widespread service, particularly in metropolitan areas. Similar to MTN Rwanda, plans start at $5 for a few GB.

Tips for Purchasing a SIM Card:
- Look for approved merchants at airports, large bus stations, and official mobile network stores.

- Keep your passport accessible, since identification is necessary for purchasing.

- Choose a data package that corresponds to your use. Consider your typical surfing patterns, social networking requirements, and any internet calls you may make.

Wi-Fi: Wi-Fi coverage is expanding in Rwanda, notably in large cities and tourism destinations. Hotels, motels, cafés, and restaurants often provide Wi-Fi connections to their visitors. However, speeds may vary and connections may be inadequate in more rural regions.

Important Note: Be aware of your home phone company's roaming costs. Using a local SIM card is often substantially less expensive for an internet connection.

19.2 Staying Connected with Phone Calls and Texting: Keeping in Touch

Using Your Home Phone Number: Calling from your home phone number when traveling might be pricey. Before you go, check with your phone provider to see what their international roaming costs are.

Using a Local SIM Card: The local SIM card you buy for internet access may also be used to make calls and send text messages in Rwanda. Rates are often far lower than roaming costs from your native nation.

Tips for Making Calls in Rwanda:
To call a Rwandan number from your phone, dial the country code +250, then the local phone number.
If you want to make overseas calls, consider getting a bundle with international calling minutes included.

Staying Connected Responsibly
Beware of Public Wi-Fi: Avoid utilizing public Wi-Fi for important tasks such as online banking. If you must

use public Wi-Fi, consider utilizing a VPN (Virtual Private Network) to increase security.

Respect Local Data Usage: Download big files or stream films over Wi-Fi whenever feasible to avoid exceeding your data limit and paying extra fees.

Following these guidelines can help you remain connected during your Rwandan experience. Share your images, get in contact with loved ones, and get crucial information while traveling this wonderful nation.

Chapter 20: Sustainable Travel Tips: Making a Positive Impact in Rwanda

Rwanda's magnificent scenery, rich culture, and indomitable spirit make it a memorable tourist destination. However, as responsible travelers, we must reduce our environmental effects and ensure that tourism benefits both tourists and residents. Here are some sustainable travel recommendations to consider during your Rwanda adventure:

1. Choose eco-friendly accommodations:
Choose resorts and campgrounds that promote sustainable practices. Look for LEED (Leadership in Energy and Environmental Design) certifications or ask about their environmental efforts, such as water saving, renewable energy usage, and local employment.
Consider staying at a locally owned guesthouse or homestay.

2. Respect the environment.
Reduce Waste: Use reusable water bottles and avoid single-use plastics. Pack lightly to decrease luggage and limit your carbon impact. Dispose of rubbish properly in designated containers.

Respect the recommended viewing distances while gorilla trekking or on safaris. Avoid making loud sounds or quick movements that may upset the animals. Follow park restrictions and choose excursions run by ethical, conservation-focused organizations.

Conserve Water: Take shorter showers and be aware of your water use. Many hotels have water-saving measures in place; please assist them by following their recommendations.

3. Support Local Communities:

Shop Local & Fair Trading: Buy souvenirs from local craftspeople and businesses that support fair trading methods. This guarantees that craftsmen are fairly compensated for their labor while also helping to maintain traditional crafts.

Choose Responsible trips: Select trips that directly help local communities. Look for organizations that use local guides, support conservation initiatives, and give back to the areas where they operate.

Learn a Few Kinyarwanda Phrases: A few simple Rwandan greetings and phrases may go a long way toward demonstrating respect for the local culture and encouraging pleasant relationships.

4. Be culturally sensitive:

Dress Modestly: While Rwanda is growing more liberal, wearing modestly, particularly while visiting villages or religious places, shows respect for the local culture.

Ask Permission Before Taking Photos: It is usually courteous to seek permission before photographing people, particularly in rural settings.

Respect Local Customs: Be aware of local customs and traditions. Learn about acceptable conduct in religious settings and during rituals.

5. Pack Mindfully:

Bring Reusable Items: Pack reusable bags, water bottles, and cutlery to help reduce trash.

Buy Eco-Friendly Products Produced in Rwanda: To support local companies and decrease your carbon footprint, consider buying reusable things like water bottles or shopping bags produced from recycled materials.

Avoid Unsustainable Souvenirs: Stay away from souvenirs derived from endangered species or those that contribute to deforestation.

Bonus Chapter:

Adventures and Itineraries.

Chapter 21: Suggested Itineraries

This chapter presents two itinerary alternatives for experiencing Uganda, each tailored to a distinct set of interests and time constraints. Remember, these are just recommendations; you may tailor them to your interests and speed.

Important Note: When organizing your Ugandan expedition, you must get gorilla trekking permits well in advance. Permits are scarce, and trekking excursions tend to fill up fast, particularly during peak season.

Transportation Options in Uganda:

Domestic flights: Entebbe International Airport (Entebbe) provides quick access to Uganda's several national parks. Consider domestic flights if you have limited time or are going between physically distant destinations.

Uganda has a well-established public bus network that connects the country's main towns and cities. While inexpensive, travel might be sluggish and congested.

Hiring a private driver/guide allows you additional flexibility, comfort, and local expertise. This is especially useful for wildlife safaris and exploring rural locations.

Self-Drive: For the adventurous tourist, renting a vehicle provides maximum freedom and enables you to explore at your leisure. However, road conditions vary, and driving in unknown areas may not be suitable for everyone.

21.1 Short Uganda Adventure (3-5 Day):

This schedule is great for individuals who have limited time and wish to see some of Uganda's attractions.

Day 1: Entebbe and Kampala.
- Morning: Arrive at Entebbe International Airport and travel to Kampala, Uganda's capital (about an hour).
- Afternoon: Explore Kampala at your speed. Visit the Uganda Museum to learn about the country's rich history and culture. Stroll around Nakasero's busy markets or Buganda Road's artisan stores to get souvenirs.

www.ugandabudgetsafaris.com

Uganda Museum, Kampala
- Evening: Take a leisurely dinner cruise on Lake Victoria with spectacular views of the Kampala cityscape.

Day 2: Jinja and White Nile Rafting.
- Morning: Leave Kampala for Jinja, the starting place for your white-water rafting trip (about a two-hour drive).
- Afternoon: Get your adrenaline racing with a thrilling white-water rafting adventure on the great Nile River. Choose a rafting package according to your expertise level, from exhilarating rapids to serene floats.

- Evening: Relax and relax at your Jinja hotel, or treat yourself to a celebration meal after your rafting excursion.

Day 3: Visit Ziwa Rhino Sanctuary and optional beach relaxation.
- Morning: Drive to Ziwa Rhino Sanctuary, a critical conservation initiative committed to saving the endangered black rhinoceros (about 2.5 hours).
- Afternoon: Join a guided rhino trekking adventure in a specialized vehicle to see these majestic animals in their natural environment.

Option 1: If time permits, continue your trip to Uganda's western coasts and relax on the stunning beaches of Lake Victoria at a lakeside resort (about a 4-hour drive from Ziwa Rhino Sanctuary). Spend the remainder of the day relaxing in the sun, swimming in the lake, or visiting the local islands.

Day 4 (Optional for Beach Extension): Relaxation at Lake Victoria.
- Full Day: Relax and enjoy the peacefulness of Lake Victoria. Relax on the beach, participate in water sports like kayaking or

paddleboarding, or visit the adjacent Ssese Islands for a more natural experience.

Day 5: Departure
- Depending on your flight itinerary, you may rest at your lakeside resort or return to Entebbe for your departure flight (a 6-hour journey from Lake Victoria).

Transportation:
This schedule may be completed with a mix of public buses and a private driver/guide.
If you want to drive yourself, make sure you have a trustworthy 4WD vehicle, particularly for trips to the Ziwa Rhino Sanctuary.

Accommodation:
- Entebbe, Kampala, and Jinja provide a range of hotel alternatives to suit all budgets and interests.

If you want to prolong your stay at Lake Victoria, some various lakefront resorts and hotels provide beautiful scenery and leisure options.

21.2 Uganda Wildlife and Gorilla Safari (7-10 Days):

This itinerary is ideal for wildlife enthusiasts and nature lovers looking for an amazing gorilla trekking adventure.

Day 1: Entebbe and Kampala.
- Morning: Arrive at Entebbe International Airport and travel to Kampala (around 1 hour).
- Afternoon: Explore Kampala at your speed. Visit the Uganda Museum and learn about the country's rich history and culture.

Day 2: Entebbe—Bwindi Impenetrable National Park
- Morning: Take a domestic aircraft from Entebbe to a small airport abutting Bwindi Impenetrable National Park (around 1.5 hours). Upon arrival, you will be taken to your accommodation in the park.
- Afternoon: Relax and take in the spectacular beauty of Bwindi Impenetrable National Park, a UNESCO World Heritage Site.

Day 3: Gorilla trekking in Bwindi.

Pre-dawn: Get up early with a packed breakfast and anticipation for your gorilla trekking expedition. Park rangers will give you a briefing before you begin your walk.

Morning: Begin your once-in-a-lifetime gorilla trekking adventure. Hike through the beautiful jungle with skilled guides, looking for habituated gorilla families. Witness these gorgeous animals in their natural environment and study their social relationships.

Day 4: Bwindi Impenetrable National Park: Optional Activities

- Full Day: In addition to gorilla trekking, Bwindi has a range of activities. Take a nature walk around the park's various landscapes, looking for primates like chimps and baboons, or stop by the educational Bwindi Impenetrable National Park Visitor Center.

Day 5: Bwindi Impenetrable National Park and Queen Elizabeth National Park.

- Morning: Depart Bwindi for a lovely journey to Queen Elizabeth National Park (about 6 hours), stopping near the Equator for a photo opportunity along the way.

- Later: Arrive at your lodge in Queen Elizabeth National Park for a peaceful day overlooking the park's savannah vistas.

Day 6: Queen Elizabeth National Park: Game Drives and Boat Safari

- Morning: Take an exciting morning game drive in a bespoke safari truck. Explore the Kasenyi plains to see animals like as lions, elephants, buffaloes, and many antelope species.

- Afternoon: Take a boat tour in the Kazinga Canal, a natural canal that connects Lake George and Lake Edward. Observe a wide variety of aquatic fowl, including hippos and crocodiles, lounging on the shoreline.

Day 7 (optional): Queen Elizabeth National Park, Ishasha Sector

- Full Day: For an added wildlife adventure, consider taking a dedicated game drive in Queen Elizabeth National Park's Ishasha Sector. This location is known for its tree-climbing lions, which provide a unique photography opportunity.

Day 8: Queen Elizabeth National Park: Optional Activities or Departure
- Full Day: If time permits, visit other regions of Queen Elizabeth National Park or take part in activities such as chimp trekking in Kyambura Gorge. Alternatively, leave the park and return to Entebbe for your departure flight (about 6-hour journey).

Day 9 and 10 (Optional Extension): Murchison Falls National Park.
- Day 9 and 10: For a complete Ugandan wildlife experience, expand your trip and go farther north to Murchison Falls National Park, home to the majestic Murchison Falls, Africa's largest waterfall by volume. Experience boat safaris on the Nile River, game drives in search of various species, and the thunderous majesty of Murchison Falls.

Transportation:
- This schedule works best with a mix of domestic flights and a private driver/guide.

- Domestic flights save time, allowing you to make the most of your time in national parks.

- A private driver/guide assures a comfortable ride, shares useful information and insights during your safari, and skillfully navigates park roads.

Accommodation:
Uganda has a range of resorts and campgrounds inside national parks to suit various budgets and interests.
Choose resorts with beautiful sites and facilities to improve your wildlife encounter.

Contact information, locations, and maps:
- For gorilla trekking permits, contact the Uganda Wildlife Authority (UWA) at https://ugandawildlife.org/.

- Several respectable safari companies are operating in Uganda. Research and reserve your gorilla trekking and safari activities in advance, particularly during peak season.

21.3 Best of Uganda and Rwanda (10-14 Days)

This program offers the best of both Uganda and Rwanda, combining exhilarating animal encounters in Uganda with stunning gorilla trekking in Rwanda and a deeper exploration of Rwandan culture.

Day 1-3: Explore Uganda (see itinerary 24.2 for details).
Follow days 1-3 of the Uganda Wildlife & Gorilla Safari schedule (Chapter 24.2) to see Kampala's culture, go white-water rafting, and see rhinos at the Ziwa Rhino Sanctuary.

Day 4: Uganda-Rwanda (border crossing)
Morning: Depart from your Ugandan lodging and travel to the Rwandan border (about 4 hours depending on your location). Complete the border crossing procedures.

Day 5-7: Volcanoes National Park and Gorilla Trekking in Rwanda.
Days 5-7: Spend your days exploring Rwanda's magnificent Volcanoes National Park. Track a habituated gorilla family on a once-in-a-lifetime gorilla trekking adventure comparable to yours in Bwindi (refer to day 3 of itinerary 24.2). Volcanoes National

Park also provides breathtaking views and the opportunity to see golden monkeys.

Day 8: Explore Rwandan Culture and the Genocide Memorial
- Morning: Depart Volcanoes National Park for Kigali, Rwanda's capital city (about a 2-hour drive).

- Afternoon: Visit the Kigali Genocide Memorial, a moving homage to the victims of the 1994 genocide. Learn about Rwanda's history and its incredible path to reconciliation.

www.aegistrust.org

Kigali Genocide Memorial, Rwanda
- Consider visiting the Inema Art Center, a venue for Rwandan modern art, or exploring Kigali's busy marketplaces to have a personal experience of Rwandan culture.

Day 9 and 10: Optional Activities in Rwanda.
- Day 9 and 10: Depending on your interests and available time, Rwanda offers a variety of activities.

- Visit Akagera National Park for a typical safari experience, go chimp trekking in Nyungwe National Park, or take a picturesque trip to Dian Fossey Gorilla Fund's Karisoke Research Center, where Dian Fossey's work in gorilla conservation continues.

Day 11-14 (Optional Extension): Explore Uganda's Murchison Falls.
- Day 11-14: For a full East African journey, extend your schedule and return to Uganda for a few days at Murchison Falls National Park (see days 9 and 10 of the optional extension in itinerary 24.2).

Transportation:
This route may be completed using a mix of domestic flights, private drivers/guides in Uganda and Rwanda, and public buses for shorter segments if desired.
Pre-arranged transportation between Uganda and Rwanda may help guarantee a smooth border crossing.

Accommodation:
Throughout Uganda and Rwanda, there are a range of lodges and camps to suit all budgets and interests.

Opt for places that provide comfort and convenience to your intended activities.

Visas:

Most nations must get a visa to enter Uganda or Rwanda. Research your country's visa requirements ahead of time and secure all required visas before your travel.

Combining this itinerary with 24.2 enables you to see the greatest of Uganda's wildlife while also enjoying an incredible gorilla trekking adventure in Rwanda. It also provides an opportunity to learn more about Rwandan culture and history.

21.4 Rwanda: Volcanoes and Cultural Immersion (5-7 Days)

This concentrated itinerary is great for individuals looking for a shorter vacation to Rwanda, with an emphasis on gorilla trekking and cultural encounters.

Day One: Kigali, Rwanda.
Morning: Arrive in Kigali, Rwanda's capital city.
Afternoon: Explore Kigali at your speed. Visit the Kigali Genocide Memorial to learn about Rwanda's

past. Explore the lively culture by visiting local markets and art galleries.

Day 2-4: Volcanoes National Park and Gorilla Trekking
Days 2-4: Spend these days doing the highlight of your trip: gorilla trekking in Volcanoes National Park. Follow a similar routine to days 5-7 of itinerary 24.3, then go on a once-in-a-lifetime excursion to meet a habituated gorilla family.

Day 5: Optional activities in Rwanda
Day 5: Depending on your interests and available time, try visiting the Ibyiwacu Cultural Village for a look into Rwandan traditional life, learn about coffee manufacturing at a coffee farm, or enjoy a beautiful trek with spectacular views of the Rwandan terrain.

Day 6 and 7 (Optional Extension): Akagera National Park Safari.
Day 6 and 7: Wildlife aficionados may extend their stay with a safari expedition in Akagera National Park. Take a game drive across the park's various landscapes in search of lions, elephants, zebras, giraffes, and over 500 bird species. Enjoy boat safaris on Lake Ihema, which provide opportunities to see hippos and crocodiles.

Transportation:

This route may be completed using a mix of domestic flights and private cars or guides.

Domestic flights from Kigali to a neighboring airport near Volcanoes National Park save time, particularly when returning to Kigali for departure.

Accommodation:

Kigali has a range of hotels and guesthouses to suit various budgets.

Volcanoes National Park includes nice hotels and campgrounds that are well-positioned for gorilla trekking excursions.

Visas:

The majority of nations need a visa to enter Rwanda. Research your country's visa requirements ahead of time and secure the requisite visa before your travel.

This Rwanda trip focuses on gorilla trekking in Volcanoes National Park while also seeing Kigali's cultural treasures. The optional extensions provide opportunities for animal excursions and greater cultural immersion.

Remember to maintain sustainable travel habits during your Rwandan vacation. Respect local culture, support ethical tour operators, and reduce your environmental effects.

With these itineraries as a reference, you may begin arranging an amazing journey in Uganda and/or Rwanda. Explore the gorgeous landscapes, experience spectacular animals, and immerse yourself in the diverse cultures of these unique East African nations.

21.5 Multi-Country East African Adventure (Optional: Includes Kenya or Tanzania)

This chapter enables you to plan an epic East African vacation that extends beyond Uganda and Rwanda to neighboring countries such as Kenya and Tanzania. Here's a simple foundation to get you started. You may tailor it to your interests and timetable.

Sample Itinerary (14+ Days):

Days 1-4: Explore Uganda utilizing itinerary 24.2 (Uganda Animal & Gorilla Safari) or a comparable framework, with a concentration on animal encounters and cultural activities.

Days 5-7: Cross the border into Rwanda and visit Volcanoes National Park for an unforgettable gorilla trekking adventure (see schedule 24.3).

Days 8–11: Choose your next trip! Here are two choices:

Option 1: Kenya - The Maasai Mara & Beyond (Wildlife Safari): Visit Kenya's world-renowned Maasai Mara National Reserve, which is famous for its dramatic wildebeest migration and plentiful wildlife. Consider visiting Lake Nakuru National Park, which is famed for its flamingo population, or learning about Kenyan culture at a Maasai hamlet.

Option 2: Tanzania - The Serengeti & Mount Kilimanjaro (species Safari & Hiking):** Take a memorable safari across Tanzania's Serengeti National Park, observing the Great Migration and various species. Consider climbing Africa's highest mountain, Mount Kilimanjaro, for the ultimate East African adventure!

Serengeti National Park, Tanzania
Days 12-14 (and beyond): Relax on the gorgeous beaches of Zanzibar, Tanzania, or travel to other

locations in your selected country (Kenya or Tanzania) according to your interests.

Transportation:
This plan necessitates a mix of domestic flights, private drivers/guides, and maybe inter-country flights, depending on your add-on destination (Kenya or Tanzania).
Plan your flights and transportation ahead of time, particularly during high season.

Visas:
Each nation (Uganda, Rwanda, Kenya, and Tanzania) may have unique visa requirements. Research visa requirements ahead of time and secure any relevant visas before your trip.

Important note:
This schedule is just a suggestion; the choices are unlimited. Consider your interests, chosen pace, and desired animal encounters while planning your multi-country journey.

Appendix

1: Links to printable maps of Uganda and Rwanda.

While real maps are preferable, the following are links to digital materials for your convenience:

- Uganda (https://data.worldbank.org/country/uganda)

- Rwanda, https://www.cia.gov/the-world-factbook/countries/rwanda/map.

Remember, planning an East African journey needs study and preparation. Consider visa requirements and essential permissions (such as gorilla trekking permits), and plan domestic flights and accommodations ahead of time, particularly during high seasons.

By following these guidelines and modifying them to your own needs, you can plan a multi-country East African vacation that will leave you with unforgettable memories.

2: Glossary of Terms

This glossary defines some of the important concepts used in this book to help you better understand your East African experience.

Domestic flights are air travel inside a single country, which is often utilized to link large cities or national parks owing to the distances involved.

Endangered species are animals or plants that face a high risk of extinction in the wild.

Game Drive: A safari trip in a customized vehicle that takes you through a national park or reserve in search of animals.

Gorilla Trekking is hiking through a rainforest area to see a habituated gorilla family in their natural setting. Permission is required, and the experience is both physically challenging and gratifying.

Habituated Gorilla Family: A group of gorillas that have become habituated to human presence, enabling travelers to see them safely.

Lodge/Camp: Accommodation alternatives inside national parks or reserves, ranging from modest campsites to magnificent lodges that provide comfort and conveniences.

National parks are declared protected areas of land with great natural beauty or wildlife that are administered by the national government.

Permit: A formal permit is necessary for certain activities, such as gorilla trekking. Permits are restricted and must be secured in advance.

Private Driver/Guide: A professional driver with excellent experience in the area who ensures a pleasant ride, provides useful insights and effectively navigates park roads.

Public buses: A network of low-cost buses that link villages and cities throughout a nation. While cost-effective, travel might be sluggish and congested.

Responsible Tourism: A tourism strategy that reduces negative environmental and social consequences while also benefiting local communities and conservation initiatives.

Safari: A trip or excursion in East Africa, usually for animal watching. Game drives, boat safaris, and guided hikes are all possible options.

Savanna: A wide, open grassland habitat with scattered trees and plants.

Trekking: Hiking or walking across tough terrain for many days, particularly in the context of gorilla trekking.

White-water rafting is an exhilarating adventure sport in which you navigate rapids on an inflatable raft across a river. Depending on your expertise, you may choose from a variety of difficulties.